D0263439

'If you're swamped with guidance about dating, and just need a bit of practice advice to know exactly how to get started, then read on. Aukelien's guidance comes out of stories and experience, which I think will resonate with many of you.'

André Adefope, head of Naked Truth Relationships
and co-author of *The Dating Dilemma*

'*Dare to Date* steers a masterful course between the cultural relativism of contemporary attitudes towards dating and marriage, and the fanciful notion that "marriages are made in heaven". Aukelien brings together the wisdom of a practising psychologist, the faith of a committed Christian and the pragmatism of a self-help manual to give us an invaluable resource for today's Church.'

The Revd Canon Dr Adrian Chatfield,
Fellow of Ridley Hall, Cambridge

'Does your church teach on how to get from singleness to marriage in a godly way? Probably not, but this book brilliantly helps to bridge that gap. *Dare to Date* is essential reading for church members and leaders to further develop a much-needed healthy Christian dating culture. Aukelien is a Christian psychologist who understands this topic from personal and professional experience. With God at the centre, her book warmly encourages single people with really helpful insights, stories and strategies that will improve their dating lives.'

Annabel Clarke, chartered psychologist, Associate Fellow of the British Psychological Society, and founder and co-chair of the Engage Network: 'making Christian marriage possible'

'At Christianconnection.com we have been bringing single Christians together for over 16 years. But time and time again, we encounter Christians who are afraid, discouraged or uncertain on whether or how to date. Church life can often put great pressure and expectation on Christians but without offering help and support. *Dare to Date* really addresses these issues with wisdom, faith, insight, practicality and true stories.'

Jackie Elton, founder and MD of Christianconnection.com, a dating site for Christians

'This accessible and practical book is most welcome. Rooted in deep experience of how we are made as human beings, it offers a means of interacting with others and exploring romantic possibilities which resonates with culture today. Buy it, use it and discover the adventure of dating that is both godly and fun.'

Dr David Pullinger, Director and researcher into Christianity and singleness at <www.singlechristians.co.uk>

Aukelien van Abbema has a degree in psychology and philosophy and owns a private practice as a licensed counsellor in Emotionally Focused Couples Therapy (EFT). Aukelien has developed a dating course in her church, Crossroads International Church in Amsterdam, a spin-off of which is running at Holy Trinity Brompton in London. She teaches on dating, singleness and the Church throughout the Netherlands and the UK. Follow her on Twitter @avanabbema or find her on Facebook at Dare to Date.

DARE TO DATE

Aukelien van Abbema

Translated by
Erin van Santen-Hobbie

Originally published in Dutch in 2013
by Ark Media, the Netherlands

First published in Great Britain in 2017

Society for Promoting Christian Knowledge
36 Causton Street
London SW1P 4ST
www.spck.org.uk

Copyright © Aukelien van Abbema 2013, 2017

All rights reserved. No part of this book may be reproduced or transmitted in any
form or by any means, electronic or mechanical, including photocopying,
recording, or by any information storage and retrieval system,
without permission in writing from the publisher.

SPCK does not necessarily endorse the individual views contained
in its publications.

The author and publisher have made every effort to ensure that the external
website and email addresses included in this book are correct and up to date at
the time of going to press. The author and publisher are not responsible
for the content, quality or continuing accessibility of the sites.

Unless otherwise noted, Scripture quotations are taken from the ESV Bible
(The Holy Bible, English Standard Version), copyright © 2001 by
Crossway, a publishing ministry of Good News Publishers.
Used by permission. All rights reserved.

British Library Cataloguing-in-Publication Data
A catalogue record for this book is available from the British Library

ISBN 978–0–281–07701–4
eBook ISBN 978–0–281–07702–1

Typeset by Graphicraft Limited, Hong Kong
Manufacture managed by Jellyfish
First printed in Great Britain by CPI
Subsequently digitally printed in Great Britain

eBook by Graphicraft Limited, Hong Kong

Produced on paper from sustainable forests

To Anna, and every other wandering singleton who hopes to be found

Contents

Foreword

Life is about the quality of our relationships, with God and with others.

Many people today are crying out for connection. We live in increasingly fragmented societies and can find ourselves isolated. The current rate of geographical mobility has meant that more and more people are living away from the community in which they grew up and the network of relationships through which they were supported. We have more opportunities than ever to connect digitally but this has not replaced the longing and the need for more permanent face-to-face relationships.

Dating has not gone out of fashion but it has become more complicated. Hooking up for sex is one thing; dating that is both healthy for individuals and for society is another.

The old 'rules' to test the possibility of a long-term relationship no longer apply. The social conventions that allowed people in the past to explore marriage within certain boundaries have been lost. Living together and having a child without being married are no longer social taboos. In some countries, the marriage rate is at its lowest since records began. More people today are wary of commitment and, as a result, do not experience the deep trust and intimacy that the covenant relationship of marriage makes possible.

All of this has had an effect on dating. In the Church and in society at large, we need new approaches that enable people to meet, to explore if there is a growing connection between them, to form romantic relationships and to break up well if they discover they are not suited to each other. To create a common understanding between those seeking a life partner that will help make these processes a lot easier, new social traditions are needed, suited to the modern world and based on mutual respect.

That is why this book is so important. Aukelien brings years of experience counselling about relationships, as well as her own experiences of dating, to help people to find a new and better way forward. She knows that dating, with a view to building a lasting relationship, takes courage. It requires people to step out, to be proactive, to make the first move: to *dare* to date.

Dating also requires social skills, and Aukelien offers invaluable advice on how to date well, how to widen the pool of potential marriage partners and how to explore the possibility of a longer-term relationship.

We have much enjoyed getting to know Aukelien – and more recently her husband, Maarten – and talking with them around this subject of dating. We not only recognize the wisdom Aukelien brings from her professional and her personal life; we also love her passion to see single people and couples make better relationships.

We believe this book could change your patterns of dating, which could in turn alter the course of your whole life. As you read on, you will discover you are not alone in facing the challenges that twenty-first-century living brings to forming lasting, romantic relationships. But you will also discover how to take the pressure off, how to have fun and how to make good choices about other people, based on a lot more than immediate attraction.

Our hope and prayer is that through applying the practical wisdom found in these pages, many people will experience connection, friendship, love and, eventually, marriage.

Nicky and Sila Lee

Acknowledgements

I've been very fortunate not to have to write this book on my own.

My thanks go first and foremost to my love, Maarten, for his support and confidence in me.

I'm also especially thankful for the ongoing reading and collaboration with Karin Timmerman, Elise van der Kooij, Johannes Verelst and Leon Oosterhuis. Their very cool, awesome, phenomenal feedback, written between the lines, their substantive and well-founded commentary, helped make the book what it is and increased my confidence in my own writing.

This book was created through the process of leading a dating course at my church, Crossroads International Church, Amsterdam. I am so thankful for the church body and the opportunity they have given me to develop this course, in complete freedom. A large thank you is also owed to my students and friends who have heard me endlessly on the subject of this book: it is because of you that this book has become what it now is; and also that there is a book.

I'm also very thankful for the connection made with SPCK and especially Juliet Trickey, who was enthusiastic about publishing my book in the UK right away!

This English translation couldn't have happened if I hadn't met Erin van Santen-Hobbie. I'm thankful she and I became friends and that she did such a great job at translating exactly what I wanted to say. I am also thankful to Annabel Clarke of the Engage Network for her thorough editing work on the translation, to make my Dutch bluntness more suitable for delicate British ears. I love her commitment and the time and energy she puts into the Engage Network! Along with Annabel, Nicky and Sila Lee have been a great help and inspiration from the start of writing this book. They are such loving and warm people to be connected to, and I'm thankful for getting to know them.

Finally, I'm thankful to God for the doors he continues to open, such as the opportunity to write and share this book.

Leabharlanna Poiblí Chathair Bhaile Átha Cliath
Dublin City Public Libraries

Introduction
Dating from connectedness

When I was single, I felt powerless over the state of my singleness.
I thought it was something I simply had to accept, a reality I had to
learn to be satisfied with. But my perspective changed when I first
began studying singleness and the nuances of relationships, both for
my work as a psychologist as well as out of my own curiosity. Through
my research a new world was opened to me and a fresh insight
revealed: singleness wasn't something I simply had to suffer through
but was a state I could be intentional about, a subject on which I
could educate myself. In fact, singleness could be a place of growth.

Sue Johnson, a fellow relational therapist and founder of Emotionally Focused Couples Therapy, asserts that this is precisely our task:
to understand the holistic concept of love. Love is not simply a mystery that we must resign ourselves to as forever mysterious. And given
the number of divorces, Johnson adds, we cannot permit ourselves
to shut our eyes to the knowledge that is available. After all, the latest
scientific research offers us more insight into love than ever before.

The good news is that relationships do not always have to be
a complex mystery. Dating can be *understandable*, just as singleness
can. There is an increasing need for knowledge and discussion

about both, given the growing number of single people in society. A reporter once asked me if I had ever been asked surprising or unexpected questions on singleness and dating. I told her that truthfully, it had been at least a year since I had heard a new question. People keep asking me the same questions, time and time again. Much of this book is based on these conversations.

In addition to the latest research, my hope is to give people insight into *how* they date. Daring to date is not about reading all of the recent scientific literature before you step into a relationship but more about developing a basic knowledge and fundamental beliefs that provide a strong foundation for *any* relationship. This is what I hope this book gives you: a firm foundation for forming solid relationships, including dating.

We live at a time in which relationships are increasingly under pressure. Creating a firm foundation for a relationship is more important than ever. A good start to any relationship begins with 'good' dating. Dating in this book is defined as 'having an encounter with someone else, getting to know them as a person, their character, their interests. It is *not* getting to know their body, their income or their internet dating profile.'

Healthy relationships begin with *healthy* dates, dates that are intentional, meaningful. At this point it is important to understand that when I use the term 'dating' I mean nothing more and nothing less than a time and a place where a man and a woman intentionally meet, spend some time together and connect in a meaningful way. And a meaningful encounter begins with a heart connection, not a physical one. Dating is not about kissing (although this may be involved at some point), and it is definitely not about having sex. It is important to make that distinction clear, because undefined terms can lead to a lot of misunderstanding.

So what is good dating? Dating with realistic beliefs and expectations about relationships and their possibilities can only help your relationships. Open communication leads to honesty with the other person about what's bothering you. It isn't possible for another human being *always* to know intuitively what you want or to understand *perfectly* who you are.

This means that consistent communication with the other person is essential. If everybody were more conscious of how they actually date, as a relational therapist I would have much less work to do. In my job I often hear people talk about difficult things in their relationships that were actually difficult from the beginning. Maybe one person was aware of a negative thinking pattern or behaviour in the other person but pushed away any possible concerns by thinking: 'It doesn't matter that much' or 'It will change.' The issue wasn't intentionally addressed; therefore it kept on being an issue.

This book isn't just about dating (that topic in all its practicalities will eventually come in Chapter 4), but is particularly about the elements that create a firm foundation for dating. For Christians, if you can connect with God and are able to connect with yourself and love that self, then you can more easily connect to the people around you.

I use a model in this book called the 'Model of connectedness' (see Figure 1).

I divide connectedness into four sections:

- connecting to God;
- connecting to yourself;
- connecting to a community;
- connecting to the other person.

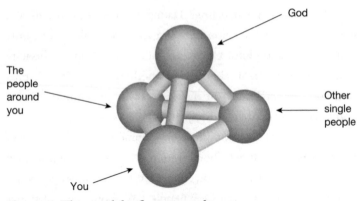

God

The
people
around
you

Other
single
people

You

Figure 1 The model of connectedness

Chapter 1 is about including God in the process of dating. In my thinking, as the Creator, God is the one who has made us as a part of his creation. I believe that he is real and that he wants a personal relationship with each of us. To me this is the foundation to all relationships; that God has created us, like him, as relational beings. I am also convinced that the principles I speak of in this book are for everyone, even for those who don't have a belief in God.

Chapter 2 addresses you yourself, and how your own issues can stand in the way of relationships. Improving your dating life begins with you! Too often we point to the shortcomings or failures of others as the cause of our lack of dates or relationships. Psychologists refer to this tendency for human beings to point to an outside source for their situation or shortcomings as *externalizing*, or *projecting*.

Chapter 3 is about dating with the support of your *team*, the people around you, married or single, who know you well. Throughout this book, I challenge you to involve your community. Not only because your community can give you unexpected insights but also because it's far more fun to involve those who know your history and character.

And finally, in Chapter 4, we come to the practicalities of dating others. How do you even begin to date when you've had some negative experiences? How do you handle rejection? And how do you know if someone is worth pursuing?

Chapter 5 considers the complexities of being in a dating relationship.

At the end of each chapter you'll find assignments and questions for further thought and discussion. It is one thing to think things over; entirely another to allow these thoughts to change your behaviour. Working through these questions and discussing the assignments with your small group or community will help you a lot with the changes you want to make.

All of the personal stories in this book are fictitious but based on the real stories of single people I have met privately or professionally. I take examples from my experience as a professional psychologist, conference speaker, workshop leader and as the facilitator of a dating course run in conjunction with my church, Crossroads International Church, Amsterdam. I also use the story of my own search for a relationship.

Over the past years I have seen how this content has helped many to find the relationship they want, and many more to find new hope and joy in the process of dating. My hope is that this book will help you find your way in the wonderful and sometimes complex world of dating; my desire is that you will find some useful insights within its pages. Relationships might be less romantic than fairy tales or movies would have us believe, but the reality of a good relationship is far more authentic, lasting and beautiful.

1 Connecting to God

'Christian singles should be better at dating than non-Christian singles,' I recently said in an interview. 'That is quite a controversial statement,' remarked a friend, which led to a lively discussion. But I still mean it. Christians *should* really be better at dating – after all, they alone have their foundation in the love of God. Unfortunately, though, this is an idea that is difficult to put into practice. Life often isn't that simple. How do you find a foundation in the love of God if you feel that there is a lack of love in your daily life? This is what I'll discuss in this chapter.

THE SMILE OF GOD THE FATHER

God loves you. Those words may sound hollow because you've heard them so often. 'Yeah, sure. God loves me like a father.' Yet it was quite some time before I could take these words and make them my own. For me, God's love was a bit abstract, vague and distant – definitely not something you could experience. And then I turned 25 and attended a Christian summer conference called New Wine.

I heard a lot of new and beautiful things about God that week, all of which seemed to be true. The whole week my head was buzzing with ideas and thoughts, and I was flooded with emotions, including pain about my singleness – pain I had hidden away for a long time. I had often complained about being single but had never really articulated the pain that sometimes came with it. I didn't dare to. Maybe I was afraid to be a burden to those around me, although I'm sure all my complaining was probably more burdensome than genuine sharing on my pain about being single would have been.

Brené Brown, a researcher in the area of vulnerability, writes that it is precisely the act of hiding our feelings that makes us most vulnerable. Although it feels vulnerable to share something you may find painful, in the end not sharing it causes you to be far weaker and more sensitive than you otherwise would be.

It was at New Wine that I decided to let go and fully participate in what God was doing. I still wasn't really able to feel his fatherly love, so I continued just to do my best. At one point, on the last evening of the conference during the singing and praying, I decided to stop worrying about it. I decided to shut off my mind for a moment, refuse to keep analysing, and just join in the singing with my whole heart. And then it happened: the roof opened up and revealed God, sitting on his throne. He looked at me and smiled. And that smile made everything right.

In retrospect, I've often thought what a strange experience that was. I'm a pretty rational, level-headed person, and because of my profession I am predisposed to doubt such a visual experience. Yet I was very certain that what happened was not just in my head but a very real occurrence. God sat there and looked at me. He smiled just as you would at somebody you know well and love even more. It was the kind of smile where you just know that everything is going to be fine. I didn't have to do anything to earn or hold on to his love. I could have been angry, laughed at him, denied what was happening, but none of it mattered. It was what it was: God was there and he was pleased with me. No matter what. End of story.

It was such an intense, life-changing moment. From that day on, the memory of his smile never left me, travelling with me through seven more years of singleness. But even this experience didn't actually make those years easier. The father-love of God isn't intended to protect us from pain or discomfort. The love of God doesn't fill in everything we're missing. If someone whom you love has died, or you lose your job or home, the pain doesn't simply go away just because God loves you. But the pain can become bearable, or at least not unbearable.

If God is Father, than what kind of child are you? To put it as Paul does, do you drink only milk (1 Corinthians 3.2)? Or should you be feeding on something more substantial as a result of having grown in spiritual maturity? Connectedness to God will lead to ongoing growth. Connecting to God is exactly what I mean when I talk about 'dating God', which we'll cover later. It means talking with him, sitting with him, listening to him. It means opening your Bible, finding your quiet space and doing life with him.

PARENTS: INFLUENCERS OF OUR IMAGE OF GOD

What about your earthly parents? Even as an adult you can still have an important and significant relationship with your parents. The exception is that they are no longer in their former role as primary caregivers. Of course, good parents are there if you need them but they're not there to clean up every mess you make. We could even go so far as to say that such an involved relationship would be, well, wrong.

In my counselling practice I regularly come across people who are still dependent on their parents. Take Ellen, for example. She came to me in the middle of a complicated divorce. Her husband had been involved in fraud in his business. Because they had joined their financial resources when they married, when he was forced to file for bankruptcy so was she, and as a result she was deeply in debt. But that wasn't Ellen's greatest complaint. What she was struggling with the most was the feeling of being left high and dry. The interesting thing was that her feelings of abandonment were not so much about her husband. Of course she was angry with him, he had let her down. She also knew that she had ignored some serious red flags in order to marry him. But her greatest pain was in the fact that her parents weren't as involved as she would have liked.

'You know,' said Ellen at the initial session, 'they *are* my parents. They are supposed to support me!' 'What would you have them do for you?' I asked. 'Why, they could do a lot. Take care of me, take me in, talk to my kids and tell them to listen to their mom, let me borrow money to get out of debt.' 'How old are you?' I asked. 'Thirty-four,' she answered suspiciously. 'Right,' I said, 'and what kind of relationship should someone of thirty-four expect of their parents?' 'That maybe I can take care of more things myself,' she admitted, somewhat reluctantly. Of course, parents may well support their adult children in such circumstances but the problem was that Ellen was still too dependent on hers, and wasn't taking enough responsibility for herself.

It can sometimes be much harder for single people to let go of the parent–child relationship, especially if they've never been married or never been in a long-term relationship. Sometimes it's difficult even when you have a really good bond with your parents. Maybe you can tell your mother anything, and your father is the best at helping you fix things around the house. Maybe you're looking for a relationship where the other person matches both criteria.

Sometimes it is even more difficult when you have a troubled relationship with your parents. Perhaps they were not emotionally available in some way or in some period of your life. You're always hoping, very understandably, to improve your relationship and therefore remain too attached and dependent on them, instead of standing on your own two feet. You may even be likely to fall for single people who are not emotionally available enough either.

How do you see God? As a father who does the difficult household tasks, like finding you a partner? You can find these words in the Bible: 'Ask, and it will be given to you; seek, and you will find' (Matthew 7.7). Many Christian singles tend to think that God will bring 'the one' into their life. They imagine he'll tell him or her to knock on your front door. Strongly put, these good Christian singles are absolutely *certain* about this. At least, they will always tell you that they believe God will *bring* them his best.

There will be times when they think that God's best requires some waiting, but you won't hear them complaining. They believe it will happen. They believe so strongly, that they are certain God will take care of everything himself. They cite the verse that everything will work together for the good of those who trust in the Lord (Romans 8.28). And they wait.

However, this approach is never stated in the Bible in terms of any aspect of life, including dating. God never says 'Put up your feet, take it easy, and relax. It will be okay. I will make sure that things will turn out the way you want. Just go to sleep and you'll see, tomorrow your fridge will be miraculously full and I'll give you your dream job and "the one" will give you a call soon.' No, actually the Bible is very consistent in this message: pray and work. Ask for blessing but do what you can. Leave your concerns in God's hands but take action too. Take responsibility.

Good parents know that they must let their children go a bit more every day. Sometimes they help support small steps of independence but often the children take the biggest steps forward themselves. Parents also know that solving each and every one of their children's problems doesn't help them in the end. So even if they're anxious, they don't say so when their beloved daughter wants to go backpacking in Africa, as their son makes the decision to move to a big city on his own, when their precious child decides to risk his or her life and go skydiving abroad.

Of course, a good parent will cry 'No!' if their child wants to go backpacking without a mobile telephone or survival kit. And of course they will help in the search for a flat in the city, or hear all about the details of the skydiving adventure, even if it gives them a near heart attack. They love their child, and as a result will help where they can with genuine interest in his or her continuing development.

At the same time, the children need to take appropriate responsibility. They themselves must make sure they have everything they need when packing their bags. They themselves must ultimately decide on this or that flat in the city, and they themselves remember to contact home to confirm they have survived the skydiving!

GIVING UP ON GOD

God is a God who is involved, the Father who concerns himself with his children. It is only a question of responsibility: are his children doing what they can themselves to live their own lives?

God is with us but we don't always involve him in our lives as we should. Herman (37), who was following my dating course, told me after one of the workshops that:

> I had given up on God. I was angry with him, thought that he had forgotten to bring me my wife. I really wanted to get married but I never met someone I thought was the right fit. I concluded that God simply did not want me to marry. My younger brother, on the other hand, has been in relationship after relationship. And he is completely careless with the women he dates. He keeps stringing them along and feeding them lines, but never commits to any of them. And he has little respect for them when it comes to sex, jumping into bed with everyone. Meanwhile, I'm still a virgin and furious. I'm thinking 'So why did I save myself all of these years? When is God going to reward that sacrifice?'

He continued:

> But when I took your course, your first assignment for us was to 'date God'. So I did it. I live close to the beach, so I went for walks. It was really peaceful alone with God. And at your encouragement I told him that I was angry with him because I felt he hadn't rewarded me with a wife for my good behaviour. Just at the moment I heard myself saying those words out loud, I realized that I sounded like an idiot. As if I could earn a partner! And how would that seem to a potential wife, right? 'Hello, I've earned you by

living a life of chastity.' Of course it doesn't work like that. So I talked it over with God and said 'I'm sorry that I've blamed you for a problem that's actually mine. Help me see what I can do about it.' I'm not going to tell you everything that God said to me then, but the core message was 'I love you, and if you decide to start dating, I'm with you.' That was a great weight off my shoulders. Now I feel much closer to God, and it's that closeness that fills me with joy.

Three years later, and this same man is engaged to be married.

God sees our value and potential more than we can see it ourselves. Where we see ourselves as dependent children, God sees us as independent adults. He is working in our lives, and at the same time we need to take responsibility appropriately too. He sees us as people who have received what they need to go on the adventure of relationship.

GOD AS LOVER

The Christian psychologist Hud McWilliams[1] argues that we should not limit our perception of God just to *Father*. There are so many ways God's love is described in the Bible. And one of them, perhaps the most exciting, is the description of God as *lover*. The book in the Bible called Song of Solomon (or Song of Songs) is about the love between a man and a woman, but some commentators also highlight how it can be read as an allegory describing God's love for humankind. Reading Song of Solomon as a love letter from God is enough to make you blush. The love described there is physical, intimate and tangible. And yet this is how God's love is described.

What do you think about seeing God as a lover? Some may protest at the description, feeling uncomfortable with the sexual connotations. Others may be a little too comfortable with a 'Jesus is my boyfriend' idea. There is a danger that people will spiritualize their singleness. They think God is the only lover they will ever truly need. But what does that actually mean?

The meaning of God as lover is different for everyone. My challenge for you is to go on a 'date with God'; to spend time discovering what it means that he loves you; to discover what it means that you are single but deeply desire to get married; to invite him into the new dating relationship you might find yourself in.

There is another element to seeing God as a lover. Everyone longs for someone who feels like a perfect fit, who understands and accepts you fully as you are. Parents can come close to this but often miss the mark. Friends can come even closer but fail to see you for all you are. Lovers come the closest but even they are broken people in a broken world, making the search for the perfect love an endless one. That's the reason why serial monogamy is so popular in our society. If your lover is missing something (after six months, or a year or two), then you simply look for someone else who can make a better offer.

The writer Lori Gottlieb puts it aptly in her book, *Mr Good Enough*, when she describes the modern single woman as someone who is always looking for the perfect man whom ultimately she will not find.[2] This woman finally sighs that she wishes she'd stayed with her first boyfriend (who by now is usually married, perhaps to someone who had more realistic expectations). She regrets having turned down her boyfriend at 24, just because she thought she could do better or that she needed to become more mature before she could really choose. This sort of regret is agonizing.

The search for the perfect lover can in some ways reflect a godly yearning. It demonstrates a desire for wholeness, perfection, for the way God intended creation to be. Our longing is for him, the perfect lover. Often we mistake this longing for someone or something else, and it takes us in the wrong direction. We may experience fleeting moments of fulfilment but actually we search for perfection here on earth that only exists above.

Men or women who think they've found the perfect partner have an even bigger problem. The day will come when they discover that the other person is 'just human after all'. Diana (26) decided after two private coaching sessions that she had accomplished her goal. She had found 'him'. He drove the same type of car and they shared the same kind of phone. They were from the same region of the country and both loved classical music. This had to be a match made in heaven; it couldn't be anything else.

'It is so amazing,' she said. 'He gets me!' 'How long have you known him now?' I asked carefully. 'Three weeks,' she answered, beaming. 'Oh, I know. That's a very short time. But I know for sure that this is it!' 'Make sure you have at least five dates,' I advised, and then said no more.

Six weeks later, at our last session together, the relationship was over. 'He wanted to go much further than I did sexually and didn't respect my boundaries,' Diana told me tearfully. 'That was the end of the road for me. I don't get it. Am I really that stupid? Why am I so hopeless?' I answered:

> You're not hopeless. You tried. Well done! And you have boundaries. Even better! It's disappointing that this didn't go anywhere. And it's completely understandable that you thought that this relationship had real potential. This is how infatuation hormones work. Now it's a matter of getting up and going again.

In Diana's case, her rose-tinted glasses came off after six weeks. If something is amiss within a relationship, this is a nice and early time to discover it. But no matter the relationship, sooner or later the rose-tinted glasses will come off, even for the happily married. That's when you finally see the real person, complete with imperfections and problems, just like you. Or suppose you do find the perfect partner but then you have a child who is not achieving as highly as you would like? What are you going to do then? Force the child to meet your perfect standards? Unfortunately, I see too many parents who are trying to do exactly that.

Many marriages get into trouble because each person is expecting perfection from the other. Couples or singles who harbour the idea that a partner should be fully attuned to their every need will be woefully disappointed. There is only one who will always love you, who sees you and completely understands what he sees, and that is God. The people around you will always be human.

Our thinking about what's 'true' is heavily influenced by Hollywood. Hollywood would have us believe that there is a soulmate for everyone, a love that is meant to be and that it is our destiny to find that person. This person will fill us, make us whole and complete us. Take the film *Jerry Maguire*, when the Tom Cruise character says to Renée Zellweger's 'You. Complete. Me.'[3] In fact the idea of 'the one' originates in the writings of Plato, where humankind is described as formerly four-armed and four-legged and then divided. Now we are, literally, eternally destined to seek our other half.[4]

Try it. Search high and low, and you will never find that mentality in the Bible. God does not promise us our own soulmate: our own Adam or Eve. God only promises to go with us in our search for a relationship. This can be confusing. Many singles believe strongly in the idea that there is one person waiting just for them. In fact this mentality is often taught! If you meet 'him' or 'her', you'll *just know*. It will be clear that this is your one, true love, the one you've been waiting for. Sometimes this can be true. Those stories exist of people who, on meeting their husband or wife for the first time, *just knew* that they had met their future spouse. There are people who say they fell in love at first sight. But there are many more people who don't have this story, yet are together and are really happy with each other. Those stories are somehow less popular, or you don't hear of them as often. But if you ask a married couple, nine times out of ten either one or both will say 'No, he wasn't really my type' or 'I had some serious doubts about her in the beginning.'

God has created us as people who have a need for the others around us. He will not fill the hole that is meant for other people. You don't need to be the kind of single person who says 'Jesus is my lover'; although some singles may think that way. You don't have to emulate Paul, remain single and become a missionary. You are free to but you definitely aren't obliged to. Understanding God's love for you, however, can be the difference between stressed or relaxed dating, hopelessness and healthy desire.

GOD'S PLAN FOR YOUR LIFE

The poem 'Footprints in the Sand' has long been a favourite among Christians. It sounds so beautiful, two tracks of footprints on the beach and then suddenly only one set of footprints, a representation of not being left alone but actually carried by Christ.

Yet within this beautiful poem lies some questionable theology. Does God really work like this? How often has life really been difficult because of your own decisions? And if you haven't made it difficult yourself, then for how long and for what reason have you asked God to carry you? When do you decide that it's time to walk on your own two feet?

Lately I've come across a parody, the title of which translated is close to: 'Dragging Your Behind through the Sand'. It tells of long, deep ruts beside the footsteps. And as the person asks God what the tracks mean, God answers 'That's where I dragged you because you refused to walk on your own two feet.'

Too many singles simply refuse to stand on their own two feet when it comes to dating relationships. I find this frustrating because there are so many independent, quality, enterprising single people around. They can enter into and maintain friendships, so they're not relationally challenged. But if you ask them about their absence of a partner, you get dubious stories in reply. Singles often have a story ready of the reasons they remain single. That can be understandable and even healthy, as long as the story reflects reality.

Annemarie (36), a client, was concerned that 'the one' had failed to show up in her life. She was angry about it, and quite sad. But, as she told me:

> I have to wait for him. Otherwise it's as if I'm receiving a gift
> from God that he's promised to give me, but in the meantime
> I get tired of waiting so I open something else. If I do that,
> then I'll miss the real gift.

'So there is one big gift. And if you wait and turn down the other gifts, then you have earned the greatest and truest gift of all?' I asked, to be certain I'd understood. 'That's right,' she said. She looked at me with an expression that dared me to say anything further. 'Okay', I said. 'It sounds like winning the lottery. Each time you hope a little more that all of your small sacrifices will result in the ten million jackpot.' 'It does kind of feel that way a little,' she said, 'and the odds seem very small.'

The basis of many of these thought patterns is fear. To be afraid to make the wrong choice is actually the basis of the fear to commit. In the next chapter I will go deeper into this topic, but for now it's important to know the role that fear plays. These fears are understandable but they are not biblical. God never says 'Seek "the one" and you shall find him or her.' Seek the good, seek God's heart, seek the people around you, and your partner may be among them. That is something different.

Likewise, people often think that God has one, narrow path laid out for them. They pray continually for God to tell them whether to go right or left, and they live in fear of falling off the narrow path. They think they must search for God's one, true plan for their lives. Therefore the great fear is this: 'If I make the wrong decision, I forfeit my only chance of living the life I was meant to live.'

That's a scary perspective on how God works but I am firmly convinced life doesn't work this way. God gives us far more space. He doesn't give us a narrow path but a wide open field.

God gives you a framework – the Bible – to work with in planning your route. As long as you stay within that framework, you'll be fine. This is also true in relation to the person you marry. There are parameters but he calls after us if we wander too close to the edge. Within this framework, much more is possible. There is no one, perfect route, but a place of freedom where it is safe to make our own choices.

BIBLICAL DATING?

What in the world is biblical dating? On the one hand, it sounds a bit ridiculous to label an activity as 'biblical' when it did not exist in biblical times as it does now. We don't talk about 'biblical car driving', for example. On the other hand, there are biblical principles that we can apply to dating, just as we can apply to other behaviours, such as driving. There are dos and don'ts. Just as we want people to learn responsible rather than irresponsible driving, so dating is something to learn to do carefully and with skill. It takes skill and care to consider your own heart as well as the heart of another.

Twenty years ago, a movement began in the USA known as the 'courtship movement'. Throughout American high schools and Christian universities, spiritual leaders looked for ways to help adolescents wait for sex until marriage. They were called abstinence preachers. It was well intentioned, and the idea was this: keep young people away from sex and dating in order to keep them from sinning. Joshua Harris, a young married pastor, then wrote the well-known book *I Kissed Dating Goodbye*, which echoes this teaching. Set in the American context, he describes dating as having one relationship after the other, giving your heart away time and again.[5] So dating, in his view, is getting to know someone and jumping right into relationship mode, until you have doubts and then you jump back out of it. His book is therefore a plea against dating, especially sex within dating.

That sort of dating in fact is both unhealthy and not helpful. But I don't like Harris's 'solution'. He proposes courtship as an alternative to dating. He describes courtship as only moving on to date someone when you are ready for a lifelong commitment, and avoiding romance before God tells you you're ready for it. It is the intentional process of discovering whether marriage is the goal of the relationship, seeking God's guidance throughout the process. Courtship doesn't begin until both parties agree to start courting each other. It usually involves asking the parents' permission to do so, and involves supervised dates.

There's nothing wrong with seeking God's guidance throughout a relationship. In fact I think you should always continue to seek God's guidance, also when you are married. The flaw of the courtship system, in my opinion, is the amount of commitment and intentionality required at the very beginning of a relationship. It makes dating almost into an engagement, and the way it is promoted puts so much pressure on the process of dating that it can be daunting for Christians even to begin.

The idea of courtship does have some value. Just as an alcoholic does better to abstain from alcohol altogether so that he or she doesn't fall into former patterns of behaviour, the avoidance of anything potentially dangerous or harmful can be a solution. Have you been overweight? Stay away from chocolate. Have you ever been in a car accident? Don't get into a car. Have you ever been mugged? Stay at home. These are simplistic solutions to the danger you were so afraid of, and you can try to exercise control through these avoidance methods.

But through avoidance something else happens. You begin to live your life led by fear. That isn't to say that fear can't be useful. It can sometimes protect us. Without fear we would be lucky to survive another half hour. Healthy fear makes us cautious. Unhealthy fear, however, can have a paralysing effect. Dating can be scary. You run the risk of your heart being broken. And how obsessed is our culture with a broken heart? Broken hearts are fodder for artists. Countless songs are about broken hearts. But is all of this obsession necessary?

Your heart is a muscle, not a bone. Think about it. Bones can break but muscles are much more flexible. Of course, muscles can tear but in principle they are strong. You also run a risk by not using a muscle. Without use, muscles become weak and small, almost unusable. Give a grown man with a broken leg two weeks of bed rest and he will lose a significant amount of his muscle mass. So it is with your heart when it comes to dating. You must have the courage to continue to use it. If you're a person who eventually wants to marry, then the continual use of your heart is vital. Healthy dating will be good exercise for your heart if it involves God's biblical principles.

We must all face the fears and tensions of dating. We must choose, and grow. And with this comes the possibility that the choices we make will result in disappointment. The perfect choice does not exist, and life is not so easily controllable. Instead of searching for an ever more perfect way to choose, it is better to embrace the reality that we will not choose perfectly, that life is not free from disappointment. What does help, however, is basing your choices on God's wisdom. That's what dating with God is about.

We would do well to take Jesus' example, recharging in the presence of God to provide the rest we need to continue the adventure and challenge of dating. Jesus often withdrew to 'date God', to pray and connect with his Father in heaven. This gave Jesus both strength and rest. You regularly read of this in the Gospels. In this sense you can learn from Jesus in how he behaves as a single person. Regular retreats to be alone with God are good for your spirit. Not only do they give rest, they also help you stay focused on the truth that you are loved as you are, with or without a partner. Your life serves a larger purpose than getting married and having children, and taking your place in his coming kingdom is more important than where you end up relationally.

It is interesting to note that Jesus surrounded himself with good friends he referred to as brothers and sisters – with whom he shared life. That is something you as a single person can take as an example. Even in paradise God proclaimed: 'It is not good that the man should be alone; I will make him a helper fit for him' (Genesis 2.18). Just because you are not married doesn't mean you should live life alone. Jesus shared his life openly with his friends, male and female. He surrounded himself with mother and father figures, friends and children. He didn't concern himself with age, gender or nationality; he took the opportunity to relate to people as they came.

Throughout the writing of most of this book, I have based myself in a convent called Emmaus Abbey. My view is of tall, old, beautiful trees; I can hear birdsong and every now and then distant sounds from within the building. In a room next door, a friend of mine is also working on a book. It is peaceful here; everything is cooked and cleaned for us and we've been able to escape the daily stresses of life. We're both able to work twice as fast as we could at home.

The sisters of the Abbey come together to form a whole within their religious order. Their togetherness strengthens their individuality and helps them thrive as a community. The presence of others does something to us. Jesus knew that. He sought community everywhere he went: from his brothers, to the people he came into contact with, to his heavenly Father. Human beings are human beings because of the contact they make with other human beings.

JESUS AND DATING: BEYOND SUPERFICIAL ASSUMPTIONS

Jesus never had a special relationship with only one woman but did seek female companionship. Despite his mission, and the corresponding need to remain single, Jesus did not avoid contact with women. He could have married if he wished. Perhaps that would have even been easier in some respects, in his culture.

But the important thing is to see how he interacted with women. This was completely countercultural. Jesus, an unmarried man, related to both married and unmarried women. He conversed with them, ate with them and let them wash, kiss and anoint his feet with oil. Even if the women were prostitutes, he treated them as equals. He didn't fear them; on the contrary, he came close to their hearts and shared his own heart with them.

Jesus never made superficial assumptions or judgements about people. He saw people's hearts and not just their appearance, and had a way of relating to people that I envy. He was completely free of all of the conventions, so pure and direct and completely without timidity.

From Jesus you can also learn the importance of keeping an open mind to those you meet along the way, instead of being too quickly selective based on someone's physical appearance, personal history or marriage potential. Try to begin dating with a heart-to-heart conversation. I realize this is a completely different perspective – so many people come into dating with a list in their hand and criteria in their head. They're not dating from a sincere interest in another human being but from a predetermined checklist.

Dating with a checklist is not dating to get to know the heart of another person, rather dating to measure the value of a person based on their CV. In reality that's not a true encounter, but meaningless and unfair dating.

Miriam (31), whom I coach, told me about a man who had asked her out. They had met through a dating website. 'So, okay,' Miriam told me, 'he wasn't someone I would normally . . . but everyone should be given a chance.' I started to laugh. 'What do you mean he wasn't someone you would normally . . . ?' She sighed, hesitating. 'I'm just so tired,' she finally said, tears springing into her eyes. 'Hopeful each time, analysing each time, wondering if this could be "it".' 'When I think about his level of education, which is lower than mine, and the fact that he's younger, and my instinct tells me to "write him off",' she admits.

Miriam went on the date anyway and it turned out to be quite a significant encounter. However, it took a while before the relationship was able to progress, because after the first date Miriam called me in a panic. 'I turned him down for another date. I did the right thing, right? Tell me I made a good decision.' But I wasn't going let her off the hook that easily. 'Tell me why you said "no" in the first place,' I pressed further.

Then the whole story poured out. She had agreed to meet him at two o'clock in the afternoon. The weather was nice so they decided to cycle around a bit. In the end they found a sunny spot at a beautiful waterfront café. They sat there for two hours, talking about everything. 'I've never told someone so much about myself on the first date,' Miriam said, shocked.

After two hours had passed, they decided to go for a walk on the path on the other side of the river. The man in question, James, had conveniently already checked the ferry times, although Miriam didn't realize this until months later. There, on the other side of the river, they found themselves even deeper in conversation. 'James kept asking good questions,' said Miriam, still slightly panicked.

But Miriam kept with it, also inquiring about James. And guess what? James had big plans for his future. He had a good job in the Netherlands but wanted to do missionary work in Asia. And this, I realized, was the impetus for Miriam's panicked state. 'I can't do that! I can't live in the middle of nowhere!' she said indignantly to me. 'Nope, I've thought about it, and that is not me.' 'Whoa!' I said into the phone, 'Tell me first how it went.' 'Well,' she mumbled, frustrated, 'after we talked about his goals, we went back to the café where we had begun and talked a few more hours.'

'So if I understand this correctly,' I said, 'your conversation continued from two o'clock until seven?' 'Uh-huh.' 'So you're saying you talked to this guy from two until seven?' 'Yeah,' she said, taken aback. 'And you had fun?' 'Yeah, but.' 'And you can be yourself with him, you feel safe? And you can be open about yourself without feeling strange?'

> Yeeees. But he wants to go to Asia! I've been thinking a lot about it and it just doesn't seem smart! He's completely not my type, he's younger, he's less educated. He needs the right woman who wants to go with him to Asia! Someone whose life mission is to move to Asia!

Miriam began to take on a defensive tone. 'Do you want to hear my opinion on this or not?' I asked firmly. There was a long pause. 'Okay,' sighed Miriam. I continued:

> Right. I've listened to many of your dating adventures by now. And every time you've found a thousand 'good' reasons

to turn down the guy after one date. Yes, at least you're going on dates. Great job! But – you've not really given anyone a chance. You've let them go, one by one, for trivial reasons. One is too short, the other too skinny, one lives too far away, or has a strange accent. But those are actually lame excuses. Go out with this guy again. Give him another chance.

There was a long pause. Finally Miriam sighed 'Okay.' But the result was beautiful.

Miriam spoke to James and told him why she didn't want to continue dating him: Asia. That sole fact was making her hesitate. James listened. He understood. Luckily he was not so self-absorbed as to be intimidated by her doubts. He even admitted that it wasn't that fair of him to challenge her with that kind of information on their first date. And it certainly wasn't his intention to make her uncomfortable or pressure her to do something she didn't want to do. Her honesty helped James to see the effect his words had on her. And his openness had helped her to be honest with him.

This is also something Jesus does: he is honest in his experiences with others but also understanding of their motivations, the underlying reasons for their behaviour. Sometimes he is surprisingly direct, at other times surprisingly tender, but he is always clear. So often in dating we are focused on finding things out about the other person, and aren't open about ourselves. And so often our misconceptions turn out to be based on our own prejudices, if we're honest with ourselves. Miriam thought James would want to drag her off to Asia in a year or two, or as soon as he got the chance. But the reality was more nuanced. Miriam couldn't discover that until she was open about her fears and gave James a chance to answer.

SPEAKING THE TRUTH IN LOVE

Jesus always spoke the truth in love. He was wise about what he said, and when he said it. He was also humble. We might find it challenging to hear what people think of us, but on the other hand, feedback can help us grow.

If our lives are really rooted in connectedness with God and his unconditional love for us, and connectedness with a supportive community, we can grow in our confidence to seek, receive and give feedback in a godly way.

Jesus didn't come to pat us on the shoulder and then leave. Verbally, he could deliver a really tough message straight to the heart, but in love. Take the example of Zacchaeus, the tax collector. Jesus ate with him, talked with him, listened to his problems and considered what he said. But he was also searingly honest in his dealings with Zacchaeus, in a loving way. 'What you're doing isn't right,' was the message; 'It's morally wrong' (Luke 19). He said something similar to the woman at the well: 'The man whom you're now with is not your husband' (John 4.18). Jesus confronted this woman with what everyone was thinking but dared not say. Instead of avoiding her, he chose to come closer.

In healthy community there needs to be both kindness and honesty. So how might this apply to what we share with our single friends? 'I think I know what she keeps doing to contribute to her ongoing singleness, but she doesn't ever begin the conversation herself. So I keep my mouth shut!' a friend recently told me. 'She doesn't admit that she's tired of being single but I know that she definitely feels that way. But as long as she doesn't open up about it, then I don't feel free to address what I see.' If we have rightfully earned someone's trust, after prayerful thought, it will sometimes be appropriate to speak the truth in love in a way that will be helpful for him or her. Do this very wisely though, as challenge without rejection is a difficult skill to master!*

Honesty is an important basic principle of dating. Openness involves feedback about your motives for either rejecting someone or being willing to discover where a relationship might take you. This was definitely the case with Bart (28), an open, cheerful man who always asked the women he dated for feedback.

Once Anna, a friend of mine who had dated Bart, confided in me that she'd become tired of his constant chatter. But instead of being honest with him, she told him 'I've decided to date other people with whom I think I'm more compatible.' This was Anna's polite way of telling Bart that she enjoyed her other dates more. 'But I didn't get off so easily,' Anna continued. To his credit, Bart asked for clarification: 'Do you have any feedback for me?' Anna said:

> Those were his exact words. I was impressed, *so* impressed that I almost regretted rejecting him. I didn't think there was something wrong between us but rather that, to be honest, he was too extroverted for me. And of course neither of us could do anything about it, but for me, because I'm so introverted it just didn't feel right.

Whether Anna was correct in her assessment of Bart as not a good enough match, she could never know. For Bart, though, she had given him a clear answer he could build on. Since then, he has found a woman who is just as extroverted as he is. They

---

* I do realize that feedback is easier given in the Dutch culture. Expat friends of mine call it offensive at first but refreshing over time . . .

have great fun together. In the end, he is thankful for Anna's 'no' because he is happy with the woman who has said 'yes'.

THE APOSTLE PAUL AND DATING

But then what about Paul, the other exemplary single? Didn't he say that it is better not to marry?

Paul himself had probably been married; otherwise he could have not been a rabbi. Rabbis were married men in those days. It is speculated that perhaps he was a widower. In any case, at the time of his writing, Paul was living as a single man. He encourages his audience to live 'as I live' but doesn't say 'never marry'.

We must remember that in 1 Corinthians 7, Paul is addressing a group of people whose Jewish backgrounds exalts marriage as the ultimate goal: you had to marry and you had to have children. This was a sacred duty, the only way to contribute to the coming of the Messiah. To stay childless in a Jewish marriage was extremely undesirable; in the Jewish mentality, not only were your house and heart empty but you were cut off from the line that could eventually lead to the redeemer.

However, Paul knew that the Messiah had already come. The weight of this truth and what it meant for daily life didn't appear to have fully infiltrated the beliefs of the early Christian community. Actually, this is Paul's greatest message: the Messiah, Jesus, has already come! And that changes everything. The consequence of this realization was that it doesn't matter all that much if you marry or not. You don't need to marry anymore to be a part of the Messiah's line, a part of the kingdom. Single people are also welcome. This was the core of Paul's message, a completely new message for its time. And it was revolutionary. Singles now belong just as much as married people. Don't want to marry? Fantastic. But you're also free to choose, and if you do marry, you haven't done anything wrong.

In 1 Corinthians 7, Paul explains the pros and cons of staying single. 'Yes,' writes Paul, 'it is better not to marry. For single people I give this advice: stay single. Because then you have time and energy of your own to invest in God's kingdom' (paraphrase mine). The choice not to marry is a legitimate one. There are evangelical Christian denominations that interpret marriage as God's mandate for everyone. It some cases it's even seen as unethical to refuse a man or woman who wants to marry you. Nonsense, says Paul: you are free to *not marry*.

It is never Paul's intention to forbid marriage; it is only that he's saying that to be single is more convenient, that your hands are freer without a wife and children. Such was Paul's own experience. He adds in a very practical tone 'But it is better to marry than to burn with passion.' Most people do not seem made for celibacy, at least not for their whole lives.

The women in the convent where I write are women who have chosen another way to live. Some of them have been married, having chosen the convent life at an older age. Celibacy suits them for their current season of life but hasn't always been their reality. The biblical message is that sex belongs with marriage. That means that a single (unmarried) person best chooses a celibate life. The correct definition of celibacy is not a decision against sex in general but against having sex outside marriage. Because of this, Christians living within God's biblical framework choose abstinence for as long as they are single.

Paul was an extremely dedicated man, choosing to pour all of his time and energy into kingdom work. He could have looked for a (new) wife. He could have used all his free time simply to meet friends in a pub or go on a ski holiday, or whatever the first-century equivalent of those was. Instead, he chose to live his whole life in the service of God. And apparently Paul loved his way of life, because he recommended it to everyone.

The message of 1 Corinthians 7 reminds us not to play the martyr in our singleness: 'Woe is me; I carry this heavy burden of singleness but look at the church work I do!' Rather we should declare 'I'm happy with the free time I have to commit myself to work that honours God and suits me well.' Therefore in the period of time that you're single, you can choose how and where to invest your time in the kingdom. Any relationship, no matter how much fun, takes time and energy, and with the addition of children, that is even more the case.

In summary, Paul is saying that there are advantages to being single, but if you want to get married, then go ahead.

GENESIS

The messages we hear all around us in society are often that marriage is temporary, restrictive in its monogamous nature or confining in its unconditional commitment. On the other hand, often the Church's message is that God's love is nowhere more visible than in a marriage. The first set of messages is a lie. The second, an oversimplification.

Paul's position on the freedom to be single wouldn't have been appropriate in the Old Testament. If you take a look at Genesis, you see that from the very beginning God made man as a relational being. And still he allowed Adam to feel the initial sting of loneliness: 'But for Adam there was not found a helper fit for him' (Genesis 2.20). Even in the perfect pre-fall conditions of Eden, Adam is alone and feels it enough to mention it. Thus, in that perfect paradise, Adam was the first single person.

To feel alone in your single status is not a sin, nor is it the result of the fall. Adam was alone in perfect paradise, and sin had yet to make its entrance. I recently read an article in a national Christian magazine about singles who were polled and ranked themselves on a happiness meter.[6] No one scored as 'extremely unhappy'. And even the 'somewhat unhappy' category wasn't chosen. Everyone scored themselves as 'fairly happy' or higher. This is an interesting finding, and I would guess that those singles polled didn't tell the whole truth.

In fact other research shows that 40 per cent of non-Christian single people report that they regularly feel depressed. Some even reported feeling severely depressed.[7] It is possible that Christians are 'happier' than non-Christians, but could it also be that Christians feel less able to admit to being unhappy, because they feel they ought to be 'content in the Lord'?

Research from the UK Office for National Statistics shows that just over 68 per cent of people who live alone consider themselves happy. Compare this figure with the near 73 per cent of people who cohabit or are in same-sex relationships, and over 78 per cent of married couples who call themselves happy. Research conducted by Single Christians has shown that one of the factors that make people in a relationship happier is age. For people aged 18 to 25 there is no difference in happiness between those with or without a relationship. People over 25 are happier with a partner than without, and that is even more the case with people over 45. It also appears that those with a lower education have more difficulty as singles than those with a higher education.[8]

Revealing that you're not exactly happy with your singleness is still somewhat of a cultural taboo. In order to change, in order to be truly motivated, you've really got to want something different. And your motivation is often linked to the amount of satisfaction or dissatisfaction you feel with your current situation.

ASSESSING YOUR CURRENT POSITION

If you're able, sit down and make a list of all of the new single people you've met in the past four weeks. Make sure you write down the names of those you don't know well but could be interested in getting to know better. How many are on the list? What does this exercise do to you? If you're staring at a blank piece of paper, then you know that something is not right. If you want to get married eventually, then you have to meet people.

This exercise can be an eye-opener. Most people don't feel the immediacy to marry if they're still in their twenties. There are also many single people in their thirties who would like to be married but won't marry until they're into their forties. And so on. The question is not just if you're fed up with being single right now but if you're fed up with the long-term picture.

Many singles pack their schedules with activities in order not to feel alone. Fine. God also kept Adam quite busy for a while, naming the animals. Distraction is healthy, but only in moderation. You also need time for reflection, for contemplation, for the awareness that if you want to be married in five or ten years, there are changes you must make in the here and now. If I stay in the same pattern, my chances of meeting someone remain pretty small.

Adam could do nothing to change his circumstances. Women didn't yet exist and he didn't really know what he was missing. But his solitude was explicitly noted and classified as an undesirable situation. 'Let us make people,' God had said, before he made Adam – *people*, plural. And when Adam finally encountered Eve for the first time, the Hebrew indicates that he cried out, in effect: 'Finally, someone for me, my companion, my friend, my love!' He didn't react apathetically with an 'Uh, yeah, you're okay' or 'Maybe we can meet up for a coffee sometime.' No, he said: 'This at last is bone of my bones and flesh of my flesh' (Genesis 2.23). Sounds good, right?

THE CREATION OF MARRIAGE

The longing for a relationship is a healthy, God-given desire, placed in humankind at the beginning of creation. When Eve was brought to Adam, his cry was something like 'For me! Someone who is like me! Amazing!' Talk about something to celebrate! And despite the unforeseen difficulties they would face together, God blessed the togetherness of the first two people. He charged them with the responsibility to have children and care for the earth (Genesis 1.28). The reality of two people journeying through life together was God's idea, but just how they were going to do it was up to them. God had given them choice and intellect to use. Because of this, the way it turned out didn't mean that it was either all plain sailing (good times), or a bad idea to be together (because of the difficult times). Just as myths can exist among married people about the 'happy single' or 'desperate single', many singles also have similar myths about marriage.

Many single people want to believe that marriage is a fairy tale. They know that this is nonsense but deep down they refuse to accept that marriage can be less than that. 'When I get married, then I'll finally be happy,' sighed Anna, the friend I mentioned above. 'I know that it doesn't really work that way but I would love to be married. It seems so amazing.' Married friends of mine often say 'Sure, marriage is incredible but it's also an investment. And it's uniquely challenging.' Sometimes people even say 'It disappoints me. I expected far more from of it.' This helps mutual understanding, and gives single people a fuller picture of marriage.

For those of us who are married, let's not just leave it at 'It's not everything I thought it would be', but finish the sentence and tell the positive other side as well. Tell the whole truth. The more honest you are about where you find yourself, the easier it will be for others to be honest. Maybe marriage is more challenging than a friendship or job could ever be. But tell the other side of the reality too: maybe you've felt more unconditionally loved by your partner than you ever have before.

As the pastor and author Timothy Keller argues in his book *The Meaning of Marriage*, one of God's intentions for marriage is as a method of confrontation. Marriage is established as a refining tool, a tool to sharpen us, to smooth our rough edges. Married people often look at their circumstances much more graciously than singles. Perfectionism can have far less room in a relationship than in the single life.[9]

When God brought Adam and Eve together, he didn't say 'You will live happily ever after.' Marriage is intended as a 'whole-making' covenant between two people, a confrontational reality, because never are you more aware of your weaknesses or vulner-abilities, of your less attractive sides or of your brokenness, than in an intimate relationship. The other side is that there is nothing so powerful as a love that says, even through all of the brokenness and vulnerability, 'You belong to me.'

Just as God had previously established when he said 'I will make a helper for him', marriage is a kind of covenant in mutual helping. I am always fascinated how two people can sit in a busy restaurant without worrying about the purse or bag hanging from the back of their own chair. You yourself have little surveillance over your bag, but your companion does. You have to trust the person with the view, just as she or he has to trust that you too are watching in case something strange happens behind them.

That mutuality is fully experienced in marriage. Not 'We'll each decide to watch our own backs' but rather 'I'll trust you with my body, my life, my well-being, my belongings, with every-thing. And I'm also going to care for you, watch over you, think things through with you. I'm going to give not in order to receive but to be together, to be connected.' If I'm too preoccupied with my own life, then I'll have too little time or energy for yours.

NOT QUITTING ALREADY MAKES YOU A WINNER

Daring to date is definitely a process. 'Seek and you will find' doesn't mean 'Seek and you will *quickly* find.' For a few people, it might even be 'Seek and maybe you won't find it here on earth.' There are often reasons why someone is still single. On the other hand, how many people do you know who are married and about whom you think 'Even *you* are married!' It's not really a nice thought but most of us can admit to having thought something similar at some time.

The problem is that many people see marriage or having a relationship as something you deserve – rather like happiness or prosperity. We identify it as 'bad luck' if someone goes through a rough time. But no one really *deserves* happiness, even if we work really hard for it. That is one of the reasons that 'dating God' is such an important start to the whole process of dating. God sees your single status as meaningful, even if that status hasn't been to your liking for a very long time. You are and will remain an equal to anyone in God's kingdom as a single person.

Still I hear many singles saying 'I've tried for such a long time but it's just not happening for me.' What an enormous frustration. Despite the frustration, I would encourage you: *never give up*. Keep hope alive, even when you want to give in. Even when you're 80, dating is still possible. Persevering is not really a solution but it is a means towards achieve a goal. It is just as when you continue to apply for jobs: you may have to settle for a different type of work or salary from your original goal, but in the end you will find a job.

So it is with the search for a partner. Maybe you have to compromise some of your requirements or romantic ideals, but if you seek, so shall you find – not if you quit, as some people claim. 'When I stopped dating, that's when I found him!' That's what Simone (46) told me. 'Really, though, you have to just stop looking. Then your focus is on other things, and that's when you'll find him.' Simone isn't the only one to claim this. I know more people who talk about how they met their partner just when 'I was completely through and said to God, "I'm done with searching."'

If I question further, they always appear to have, around the same time, made a contact via a personal profile, or met a stranger at a wedding, or begun volunteer work. So it becomes apparent that they were certainly open to dating. And maybe this time provided a new opportunity exactly because of the different surroundings, leaving them open for a new relationship.

PRAYING FOR A PARTNER

How does prayer play a role in your dating life when what you need seems so obvious? Praying is talking with God. Praying in a childish manner is asking God for everything you want and then waiting until those 'wants' are 'haves'. Praying from maturity is inviting God into everything you do, and then doing what you can as soon as you open your eyes. Sometimes you have to wait until God gives something to you but more often he helps you see what you can do and then gives you the courage and ability to do it. But even that courage is a gift. 'Work alongside grace,' remind the sisters in the convent where I write.

So how *do* you pray for a partner? Compare it to how you pray for food. You go to the supermarket to buy food with the money you've earned from your job. You work for it. And still you pray God's blessing over that bread, because you know that everything you do is dependent on his grace. Whether it is food, work, a home, you yourself must put it out there in prayer and ask for God's grace, help and provision. Then you must also do what you can to be part of the answer. One cannot exist without the other.

You can't control if the 'right' man or woman comes along. But what you can do something about is related to your desire. Your path, if you travel it with God, takes you past potentially suitable men and women. You can pray for wisdom and blessing for everything that you encounter on that path, you can bring your pain to God, as well as your anger, and your sadness for the absence of that person with whom you had wanted to share your life.

You can even, if you want, pray for the man or woman who may become your husband or wife. One woman, Elizabeth, remarked what an eye-opener it was for her that on her thirty-eighth birthday her friend said to her 'If you someday marry, he is already on this earth, you know, your future husband. He exists, breathes in and out, he may have already left for work today. You can pray for him *now*.'

Praying for your future partner may sound strange but for many people it makes a big difference. Praying for someone they may come to love is an idea on which they can focus, and it often brings rest.

Finally, you can pray for God's Spirit to lead you to find a partner; for wisdom and insight to know if he or she is standing in front of you; and for hope. Hope is an issue for many people. Hoping hurts. The older you are, the more painful hope can feel. Hope asks for courage, for trust in God and in yourself. But keep hope alive! That is an important message from this chapter: allow yourself to hope for a suitable partner, regardless of your age.

The reality is that there are some people who will remain alone. This can raise questions: 'Does God not love me?' 'Is he punishing me?'[10] Christian Connection research shows that lots of people found that unwanted singleness damaged their faith in God. If you are asking these questions, or feel angry or sad, don't deal with it alone. Share your heart with someone, a friend, pastor or counsellor. There are no easy answers to these questions but you shouldn't be alone in facing them.

But above all else: don't give up! There is still hope in finding a partner, even for people in their thirties, forties, fifties or older. Since the start of the Dare to Date project, numerous relationships have formed, including dozens of marriages. It can really happen, even if it takes a long time.

QUESTIONS FOR FURTHER REFLECTION

- Why do you think you are still single? Ask trusted friends if they think there are any things you might do differently to help you move towards your goal of being married.
- What information did you find the most important in this chapter?
- What is your mindset when it comes to dating? Where do you stand (serious; just for fun; never; often; etc.)?
- What are the pros and cons of being single?
- What is God's role in your singleness?

ASSIGNMENTS

- Go on a date with God – take a walk or bicycle ride,* sit in a coffee shop, retreat to your bedroom, whatever works best for you. Light a candle and prepare to meet with God. Share your frustrations and longings with him, ask your questions and then wait on him.
- Make a list of how many people you have encountered in the past month:
  o who are new to you;
  o who can connect you with others or whom you can introduce to your network.

---

* I am Dutch, after all; we cycle all the time.

2 Connecting to yourself

If you want your dating life to change, the first change must begin with you. Have you never dated? Or have you always had disappointing dates? Do some self-searching. Is there something about you that means you don't have much luck with dating? What part do you play in this? This chapter isn't meant to give you the impression that it's all up to you, or to place the blame on your shoulders as to why you're still single. You don't have to be perfect in order to date but it doesn't hurt to take a close look at your dating life.

YOUR RELATIONSHIP TIMELINE

Begin with the past, because in part the past determines the present. Take some time to write your history of past relationships, or make a relationship timeline. What have you experienced in your past relationships, chronologically? And how have those relationships influenced your current dating – or non-dating – life? Or maybe your timeline is blank, or practically empty with just one or two dates every few years. Consider why that may be.

Allan (34) told me during a course:

> When I wrote everything down, I noticed how often I had actually been hurt in relationships. My first relationship

lasted seven years. Seven years! But it was never a peaceful relationship. In my opinion, she always wanted me to be different from how I really was. I blamed it all on her; it was her fault for trying to change me. But when I wrote it down, I realized that I had let it happen.

What are you carrying with you, and how are these burdens influencing how you're pursuing dating? Are there areas in which you still need to heal? Often singles have been hurt from previous relationships, and no one can hurt you like someone you have let in. Especially at the beginning of a relationship, people find it difficult to create healthy boundaries, making the risk of getting hurt even greater.

That is often the end for couples, the point at which they decide that they have to break up. This is especially true for couples who are not yet married, because they find it easier to break off the relationship. But the fact is that *every* relationship faces the same types of conflicts. Maybe the conflicts are in different forms but the essence is usually the same. Often the woman feels unseen and unloved, and the man not heard or respected. Often the woman becomes angry and accusatory, and the man defensive and quiet.[1] What have you learned from your previous relationships? And what will you take into your current dating life? You might not be able to prevent yourself making the same mistakes completely but you should be learning from them. Often the sort of relationships you've had can tell you something about yourself.

Once in my work as a relational therapist, I counselled a couple I'll call the 'dream couple'. Both were tall, attractive and well dressed. Everything about them was stylish and impressive: they earned good salaries, lived in a very chic renovated building and had two beautiful children. But they were desperately unhappy. The ideal lives they had imagined when they first saw each other and began a relationship had never materialized. He constantly felt insecure under her critical eye, and she always felt abandoned by his aloof attitude. Intimacy was absent.

'In the beginning we sometimes made love four times a day,' told Emily. 'But now I'm just not interested.' She grimaced. 'Even the idea of him on top of me is repulsive.' Paul looked unhappy. 'She's as unapproachable now as she was completely available in the beginning.' 'I don't know if I want to stay in this relationship,' Emily then said. It was quiet. Paul cast a nervous glance at her and then looked down at his shoes, muttering 'She says that more often now.'

As beautiful as it had probably appeared in the beginning, to guests enviously watching the breathtaking couple at their wedding, the once seemingly ideal relationship was now in danger of lying in ruins. 'And now?' I asked. 'What is your plan?' 'I don't know,' sighed Emily. 'I want to keep trying,' said Paul softly, 'but not if you don't want to.'

AGE AND DATING

One factor in whether a relationship works well or not can be age, and people often ask me my opinion about the ideal age to get married. According to most of the relationship experts, this is around age 25 – not too young, not too old. If you marry too young there is the chance that you don't know yourself well enough to make such a big commitment, and if you're older, other dynamics play a role. You may find yourself stuck in certain patterns or behaviours, or simply the way of thinking or practicalities of single living. And after you become 30, it becomes more and more difficult to meet people spontaneously.

Am I then a failure if I'm 31, 43 or 56 and still not married? Or because I married at 21? A failure, no; facing some extra challenges, quite possibly. Because that number is not just a statistic; there's something to it. Think about it. For a mutual, balanced relationship, self-knowledge is crucial. Most have this self-learning experience between the ages of 12 and 25. Until that age, the brain is still developing and has not yet stabilized in growth. Your personality has just about finished developing somewhere between your twenty-fifth and thirtieth birthday. Unhealthy patterns that continue past your twenty-fifth year become more and more difficult to change.[2]

Many singles will admit that after they've turned 30, they've developed habits and patterns that aren't easily compatible with someone else. A girlfriend of mine, Laura, who married when she was 29, told me:

> I had the same habit every day after work of finishing my tasks and then plopping on the sofa to watch television, often for the whole evening. To me, that was normal! And then Martin came into my life. Suddenly I realized that it would be really wonderful if I had enough energy left over after work for a husband. Since then I've reorganized my work habits. I've lowered my expectations, and am less demanding of myself. This makes home a more inviting place to be in the evenings.

What Laura learned was that the habits that worked for her as a single person wouldn't work in a relationship. And in retrospect, she admits that even when she was single, those patterns weren't the best. 'I would have liked to change those patterns earlier,' she told me later. 'Then it wouldn't have cost so much energy to resolve conflicts that arose. Martin was the first person who helped me realize how weird my normal day of work and rest actually was.'

YOUR HABITS - RECOGNIZING A PATTERN

Look critically at your habits as a single person. Why do you have this or that habit? 'What purpose did those habits serve?' I asked Laura. 'Looking back,' she said hesitantly, 'I think I did that every evening just not to feel how lonely I actually was, and because I dreaded coming home every night to a cold and dark house.'

We all have our ways of avoiding what we truly feel. Emotions like sadness over what hasn't yet occurred, anger over how things have been or fears about what may or may not come are difficult to allow ourselves to feel. Our natural tendency is to avoid these feelings through distraction with any activity possible. Watching television, eating too much, meeting with friends too often, working too hard – these are all ways to stop the feelings that sometimes come with singleness.

And although these feelings are completely understandable, they don't bring you further along. For a situation really to change, you have to face that situation head on. The stark reality can help you make a breakthrough. There are lovely aspects of your singleness but there are also less attractive sides.

Laura learned from her own relationship timeline to trust her infatuations less. She noticed that she felt attracted to men who were just as perfectionistic and demanding as herself. But that also proved that these were men who were just as afraid of commitment as she was. So she had often been complaining about men who pulled away, withdrew or silently disappeared. She said: 'I've learned not to depend on my own feelings, because the men whom I become quickly infatuated with turn out to be not the sort of men I could have a happy marriage with.'

When Laura first met Martin, she found him immediately interesting; he had something that fascinated her. His calm and trustworthy manner somehow spoke to her but she did not fall head over heels in love with him:

> Now I get that *these* were the qualities I most needed in a relationship. But it made me nervous that I wasn't yet in love with him. I thought it was a bad sign. And now here I am, funnily enough, more in love than ever, even since the beginning of our marriage.

CHANGING PATTERNS

Seeing a pattern allows you to change it. Do you fall for the right kinds of people? Can you trust your own infatuations? These are important questions, especially if you're looking for the 'just know' feeling. If your feelings tend to lead you astray, the question is then whether or not you can trust them.

Try the following exercise: allow your life to play before you like a film. If you continue going the way you are now without changing your current situation, how does your life look in a year; in five years; in ten years? Is the clip you see playing before you what you want?

When I looked at my twenty-eighth year like a film clip, I didn't like what I saw when I imagined myself at 38. I had a job, a house, a good group of friends and a good church where

I felt at home. I was really quite satisfied with the choices I had made, but if I kept living in the same way, I would never come across a single man whom I didn't already know. In my work I didn't cross paths with single men, or in my church because I was always too shy to talk to anyone. Yet I really wanted to be married and have children by the time I was 38! To be single at 28 was still quite nice in many respects but it was not something I wanted to hold on to for ever.

This goes for those of you over 25. As you get older it is normal and even logical that your life follows a more orderly path than before – healthy even. If you lived the full life of a university student for ever or continued to attend as many parties as you did in your twenties, in many respects you'd be exhausted by your thirties and by your forties it would start to look strange. Yet in order to meet new people, singles you might become interested in, some of your adolescent life needs to be continued or picked up again! And yes, that is exhausting but it can very well be the reality of looking for love.

To be able to follow through on all your commitments in your working life, it is good to have regular patterns, established structures that enable you to complete what you need to do. These established patterns and structures are something else to pay attention to when you close your eyes and watch your life play before you like a film. What are my patterns? Where do I go, and why? What do my weekly rhythms look like, and is every week the same? And how many 'new' singles do I come into contact with?

Overall, most single people don't have to think long when it comes to counting the number of new singles they're in contact with. The answer Laura gave to this question was:

Zero. I wouldn't know where to meet any new guys. I work in healthcare with only women and one married man. I have my set group of friends in the church, and all of my friends are either married, or they're single women.

The follow up question is: what do you think of that number? If it's zero like Laura, why is that and is it okay with you? Often the answer is something along the lines of Allan's:

My life is settled. I go maybe once a year on a group trip, or to a conference. Maybe I'll go every so often to meet people for drinks but when I'm at a party or something, I usually just find the people I already know. I probably haven't seen those people for a long time, so I find myself getting pulled into conversation. But even still, I'd rather not get stuck doing things this way for ever. I would like to meet new people.

CREATE MORE OPTIONS

And now we come to the next assignment, one I've taken from Henry Cloud's book, *How to Get a Date Worth Keeping*.[3] Every week, meet five new single people of the opposite sex who are new to you. For each one, you have to find out their name; have a long enough conversation with them to have a bit of an idea of who they are; they need to leave the conversation with a little inkling of who you are; and finally, they need to have some way of contacting you.

This assignment makes quite a strong impression. 'Five people? *Five* people? How do you think I'll be able to do that?!' I am used to the disbelief and sometimes anger that accompanies this question. Most of the time I just smile and say 'Yes, *five* people.

Good luck!' What people often don't understand at first glance is that this assignment isn't about potential dates or even marriage partners but about meeting other single people, pure and simple. Of course, if you meet people who are new you might find out they don't share your beliefs or they're not single. In that case, good for you – you have met someone new! But you might want to move on to meet single people who do share your convictions.

The first challenge of the assignment is to change your habits and 'traffic patterns' so that you are actually making it possible for yourself to meet new people. When I first took up the assignment to 'meet five new people per week', it seemed to be an utterly impossible task. But that didn't keep me from going for it. For three months I faithfully noted five new names each week in my journal. In the beginning it didn't always happen, but the longer I kept with it, the easier it became. The good news is, of course, that the five new people you meet don't necessarily have to be people you'd like to date. That takes some of the pressure off. The point is just to meet people; as long as you're making new contacts, whether or not you're dating or not dating them isn't the point.

I hope this is just the motivation you need to make some changes in your day-to-day life, all with the intention of creating more options to meet someone new.

The second challenge of the task is to learn from how you react when you meet new people. When Laura did the assignment for the first time, she was shocked. She thought that she had triumphed over her previous high-school fear of boys. 'But to my horror, I soon realized that I actually hadn't,' she told me the fourth week she tried. 'If I see a single guy about my age, my heart starts pounding. I blush, and I can only think "Oh, I must seem so weird and am saying the most stupid, uninteresting things." The cuter he is, the worse it is,' she confessed.

Laura's response is one I hear often, and it is as true for men as for women. People find this 'five singles a week' assignment extremely difficult. Often they find by using this method that it is far more frightening than they thought to initiate conversation with someone of the opposite sex, let alone flirt with him or her. All kinds of thought patterns and feelings emerge that they didn't even know existed. Dealing with other single people can be scary! Never are you more confronted with vulnerability and uncertainty than you are when you meet someone you might very well like. And your fear can be fed by all kinds of thoughts, which I will delve into in the following chapter.

The beauty of the assignment is that whether you meet one, three or ten new people each week, you are doing something different anyway. You learn to open up and to strike up an easy and light conversation with a stranger – a very helpful skill to master, especially when you don't live in a place that offers you lots of options for dating!

YOUR TYPE

But there can be other dynamics too that keep us stuck. You might meet loads of new people but rarely go out on dates anyway, because none of your 'options' look attractive enough to you. Usually we define someone's attractiveness by physical attributes. After all, that is the only information we have before we get to know someone better. People often say they can judge whether someone is their 'type' or not, simply at first glance. This idea of type is deeply ingrained. How often do you hear singles say that their date didn't result in much connection because the person wasn't exactly their type? And then the response of the listener is usually 'If they're not your type, they're not your type.' Case closed.

Am I right? What is this idea of *type* and where does it come from? It's so easily used but what it's usually referring to is a set of vaguely defined physical and character traits of a potential partner. Some character qualities are very important, such as honesty, integrity and openness. There are other less important qualities, such as is he or she eloquent, musical and organized? Many qualities that singles are convinced they need to have all in one partner combined are either very unrealistic or completely impossible to find in one human being.

Make a list of all of the qualities you think necessary in a partner. Without censoring yourself, include everything you have hoped and dreamed to find in another person, both outwardly as well as inwardly. Don't be critical with yourself but dare to be as honest as possible with dictating the list of qualities that you have in mind. Some people come up with a list that goes on to a second page. Sometimes the list is longer if they are older. Sometimes people can hardly come up with a list. But in both cases, a long list as well as a too short one may indicate that something is wrong.

When Laura — from the earlier story — wrote her list out, she discovered that she was focusing on physical characteristics, instead of highlighting the more important inner qualities. She discovered she was on the search for someone who was 'tall, blond and handsome'. It is important to identify some basic character and physical qualities that you think are important, so it may help to have a small mental list of what you're looking for. If you're looking for a job, you don't search through every vacancy but keep to the ones that fit your qualifications and experience. So it is with searching for a partner. Criteria can help you search in the right direction but discuss your list with a close friend – does your friend think it is too fussy and exclusive, or are your wishes realistic?

WASTING TIME?

'But if I'm searching for someone I'm going to spend my whole life with, how can I be *too* critical?' asked Laura defensively. 'That's true,' I said, 'but how can we talk about marriage if you see a guy across the room at church but don't go over to talk to him because he's not tall, blond and handsome?' 'Yes,' she said, now really peeved, 'but why should I waste my time on someone who isn't "the one"?' 'Did you have other plans for your Saturday night?' I asked her. Maybe it was a bit mean of me to say that but I was asked the same question years earlier. And I had no answer! Actually, I had once felt the same myself, but then I realized that if getting married was high on my priority list, then why wasn't I dating whoever asked me out?

Wasting time seems to be a big fear among single people. It is here that 'type' often comes into play. Many singles think that if they just know their type, then they know what they're looking for and won't waste any time. My challenge is to try to break out of that type mentality. Date someone you wouldn't normally classify as your type. And then date another type, and another, and another. And then look again at your original type. Were you right, were they really best for you? If you keep dating the same type, it's like having the same dish in a restaurant every time. Maybe it's good, but how do you know it's the best if you haven't tried the others?

Through dating different types of people, introverts as well as extroverts, athletic as well as intellectual, tall as well as short, you may eventually come across the person who is the right fit for you. You will complement each other and help each other grow. Or, as it's written in Proverbs: 'Iron sharpens iron, and one man sharpens another' (27.17).

In terms of time, how much does dating cost? When faced with the assignment to meet five people per week, many singles respond 'Yeah, but I could never do that! I have a full-time job, a busy life, friends and family to keep in touch with. I just don't have enough time.' But do you really want a relationship? Do you really want to marry? Single people need to prioritize time in their week to meet new people (perhaps travelling to different cities), and they may need to prioritize their finances to make this possible.

And yes, that can be complicated. When you live in a small town rather than in a big city, it might be much harder to 'get your numbers up'. Or when you're over 40 and everyone seems to be in a relationship, it can be much more of a challenge to find singles in your age group. But think about this practically. How much time will it take actually to be in a committed relationship? Five minutes per day, ten, or fifteen? Enough time to say 'Hey Babe, how was your day? What do you want for dinner?' Often it takes up a lot more time!

To engage someone new in conversation maybe takes ten minutes. If you set aside ten minutes per day, then by the end of the week you have saved up a whole hour to meet someone for coffee. You've got to learn to make a bit more free time in your life now, *before* you form that new relationship. Because relationships take time. And the time that you've learned to use to meet new people is never wasted, but is the time you've learned to free up in your schedule for another person. If you're learning to make space in your life now, it will be an easier transition once you begin a relationship or get married.

Our culture tells us that a relationship is all about *your* happiness, a happiness that you are entitled to. Yet dating with a type in mind is an egocentric way of dating. The search then becomes one of looking for someone to enrich your life, rather than searching for a way that you can enrich the life of someone else, even if it's only for an evening.

Time spent dating is never wasted time. Even if the date feels as though it was a failure, you have still invested in yourself, in your own relationship skills. You've crossed paths with someone of the opposite sex whose experience and way of thinking is different from your own. He or she perceives the world differently from you, finds some things important and others not so significant. The practised skill of dating allows you to stand in the shoes of another person for a little while and momentarily look at the world from another perspective. Your ability to empathize with others has the potential to grow, if you'll only give it the chance.

APPEARANCE

A woman in church named Marion, now 50, was left single for quite some years after a divorce. Until she met John, now 37, through a dating website six years ago:

> I called a good friend after the first date I'd gone on and told her 'This isn't him. He's a really sweet guy but definitely not my type. I just don't find him attractive.' My friend

told me 'Fine, but you need to get to know him better. Become friends with him.' So I did. After three months I started getting butterflies. And after five months, I began to notice that I missed him terribly when he was gone; I missed his company. Six months into the friendship, and I realized that I had fallen for him. I couldn't imagine that I had ever found him unattractive.

Meanwhile Marion and John have been married for a few years now, and laugh each time they tell this story. It doesn't bother John that Marion once found him unattractive (or that she is a lot older than him). 'She stayed with me anyway. And I think she's beautiful.'

Appearance is important in the sense that it is nice to be thought of as attractive. It is also good to look your best. Who is going to go on a first date unshowered? Of course you're careful to look good. We'll talk about that more in Chapter 4. But first pay attention to what you find really important. Nobody is perfect. After all, we're all a bit broken.

Now for the next assignment. Using the list of qualities you're looking for in a spouse, choose the five that are most important. Try choosing five character traits that you find important based on your dating experience. If 'integrity' is one of them, how do you define integrity? When should you see that quality emerge in a relationship? And how do you measure integrity if you've only met twice?

Alice (30), a friend of mine, had been dating Ricardo (33) for three months when they decided to go on a trip together. He wanted to take her on his sailing boat from Amsterdam to some islands off the coast of the Netherlands. The first day was a lot of fun but on the second day it began to storm and she noticed his mood change. On the third day she saw him assume a role as the commander of the ship as he ordered her around without a 'please' or 'thank you'. On top of his new attitude, he didn't concern himself with her well-being.

> If I was hungry and wanted to eat, I had to wait until he was hungry too. He didn't want to anchor until he had reached a specific location that he had in mind, even if there was somewhere suitable nearer by.

Apart from the fact my friend wasn't very assertive and didn't set her boundaries clearly, this is a case where someone's true nature only appeared after spending some time together. It is fairly easy to play the fun, sweet, attentive boyfriend or girlfriend for a couple of dates, but as you spend more and more time with someone, you begin to see the person's true colours. 'My eyes were opened', said Alice.

> The sweet, charming man I had known became a dictator. After that experience I wanted out of the relationship. I am so happy that I went on that trip; otherwise, I'm not sure that I would have seen who he really was. I can't imagine having married him.

Spending an extended amount of time with someone teaches you more about the other person than only short dates do, or just spending time together in the company of friends. There is, of course, in this story the tension of their being on a boat together at night. That might not be a wise decision, although they slept in separate beds. But apart from the issue of boundaries in sexuality, Alice was able to learn what she needed to know about Ricardo in order to make a good decision.

ATTACHMENT

Our type is often based on physical characteristics that can be explained by our developmental history. Alice's father was tall, blond and handsome when he was younger. Alice had a good relationship with her father, and he was an attentive parent. She was his princess, his beautiful girl. He always told her how lovely and smart she was, commented on how well she was doing. That is a beautiful thing, a father's affirmation of his daughter. But the danger for Alice was that she idealized her father, and that no man she met was able to reach such a high standard. She discovered that:

> Every time I meet a new guy, I always see the image of my father before me in his younger days. And the guy always falls short. 'Not handsome enough', I think. I don't like this about myself, it's so arrogant, but still . . . if I'm honest no one seems good enough.

Michael, 36, recognizes this same tendency. 'I fall for brunettes,' he said.

> It's always been that way. My friends make fun of me. But I've branched out and even started dating a woman who's blonde. It actually took some getting used to. I had a difficult time finding her pretty, so I decided to talk to my therapist about it. And what emerged from that conversation was that my mother, a brunette, was often depressed during my childhood. Because of that, she was often inaccessible, even though I longed for her. My aunt took care of us often, becoming the accessible mother figure in my life. But she was blonde. My therapist explained that I continued to long for the connection with my mother that I had missed in my youth.

So that was the origin for my preference for brunettes. My
therapist cheered when he found out I was dating a blonde,
and said 'Good for you! This is a good remedy.'

There may be a deeper layer under the physical traits we prefer,
and this layer has everything to do with bonding. Bonding is the
process of intimately connecting to another. If everything is healthy,
this happens between babies and their parents, but bonding also
plays an important role in romantic relationships. Often, a fear of
commitment comes from an insecure attachment in childhood.
Psychologists used to believe that if you began life without secure
attachments, then you were destined for a life of unhealthy con-
nections. Fortunately, researchers and therapists have retracted that
belief. From research now we can see that even those who weren't
well attached to their parents as children can form good attachments with their partners as adults. This is an important finding
that provides hope and possibility for many of us.

Some people think they need years of therapy before they
can begin a healthy relationship. They say 'You've got to love
yourself first.' The reality, however, is that loving yourself very
often is connected with loving another. It can sometimes be
surprising to see yourself through the more gracious eyes of a
partner. You don't have to be perfect to be in a relationship. Yet
people – rightly – often look for emotional stability, maturity and
trustworthiness when dating, so to work on these qualities before
and during the process of dating is always helpful.

Often I receive well-intended advice from people who
know I am writing *Dare to Date*. 'You've got to read this book by
So-and-so. It's about learning to accept yourself, which is really
important. Then and only then will somebody come into your

life.' Of course it's important to love yourself. But loving yourself goes hand in hand with loving God and loving your neighbour. One isn't separate from the other. The process of dating can often help you to love and accept yourself. Alice noticed that as well. When she went on a date, she was very careful to arrive on time, because she felt promptness showed the man respect. Men who were regularly late, especially for something as important as the first date, made Alice resentful. She discovered that promptness was a quality she valued, and not one on which she was willing to compromise.

Stay true to yourself. This is particularly important in dating. Investing in yourself also benefits your dating life. When you find the right balance, you'll appreciate your dates more. If you feel secure with yourself, it is easier to feel safe with other people. And it is easier to walk away if you don't feel safe. (Henry Cloud and John Townsend's book *Safe People*[4] gives good advice about this.)

A friend of mine, when asked to describe his ideal partner, said beautifully 'Someone with whom I can feel both free and safe.' That sense of freedom and safety is probably among the most important criteria. And that feeling starts with you. When you can set your boundaries in such a way that you can protect your own safety and freedom, you can in turn give that same sense to someone else.

GREAT EXPECTATIONS

Do you have a realistic picture of what it means to have a relationship? What do you expect on a date? So many single people have very high expectations, and so the date had better be pretty spectacular. One of the eye openers in Henry Cloud's book *How to Get a Date Worth Keeping* is when he writes: 'Forget about marriage.' What he means is, forget about marriage as *the goal* of dating. Concentrate on simply meeting another person. Look for who the person really is instead of making a rating on his or her potential suitability as a spouse.

A friend of mine spoke about how on the way to his dates he couldn't stop thinking about how he would come across, how closely his date would pay attention to his table manners or if he would have enough to talk about. I myself would end up with thoughts like 'What am I going to do if he isn't "the one"?' Both of us were expecting to know immediately after the date if we would marry that person or not. The result was that neither of us arrived at our dates relaxed but rather felt a pressure that was no fun for anyone.

In addition, the example that you have from your parents' marriage also affects your expectations. If your parents were always relatively happy together, you may quickly find yourself idealizing marriage. You see, for example, how your father relates to your mother and think: 'I want that too.'

Alice explained how one day she told her parents 'It's your fault. You are so happy together that it's made it impossible for me to find someone I can also be so happy with. You've set the bar too high!' Her father responded:

> All right, but what you're forgetting is that we've been married almost 35 years. Of course we're good together but it's taken us that long to learn how to relate to each other. Most of all, don't forget that each of us has had time to develop both professionally as well as personally. The men you meet are earlier in that development; they haven't had the time yet!

'That was solid feedback,' Alice told me later. 'Yes, I may want a man who knows himself and can take care of me but I also need to remember that he, like me, is a work in progress.'

The other side is that sometimes your expectations can be negative because of what you've experienced at home. If your parents have a broken marriage, it becomes more difficult to believe that you can have a happy one. Here, fear of commitment can play a greater role than it should. It is good to be aware of such feelings. Fear of commitment is a very healthy fear, meant to protect you from entering the wrong kind of commitments. But too much fear, just like anything else you have too much of, can be unhealthy. This extreme fear can keep you from really living life, from really going for something. Often people who have been married for longer say:

> I actually can't remember why I chose to marry him (or her). We know each other so much better now than we did then, and we're still getting to know one another. It was a step of faith to marry, and remains a step of faith to keep investing in one another throughout our marriage.

You must admit that it is a bit arrogant to assume that after a date or two you know if you've met the person you will marry. How many good men, and how many good women have you rejected after a short time, even though there was nothing you truly objected to? Or because their hair wasn't right or their shoes were ugly?

Always to be on the search for something better or different is human. And with more women than men filing for divorce in the Western world, the challenge not to be too picky seems particularly aimed at women. But men have different ways of being picky. Where women are actively seeking to improve the relationship they have or are striving to find one, men can become passive while secretly hoping for things to improve or to find just the right one. 'She just has to be really pretty, smart, have a good career. Oh, and she needs to be sweet and a good cook,' was the response from a friend when I asked him why he was still single. 'So I'm still looking.'

The author of *Would Like to Meet*, who wrote under the pseudonym of 'HopefulGirl', argues that the type of perfectionism many Christian singles are displaying in their search for a partner is related to the message many are hearing in church. 'The church teaches that God has a perfect plan for our lives, and that we shouldn't settle for something second best,' she writes.[5] As a result, you develop a sort of consumer mentality: it can always be better. You aren't able to see the person you're with very clearly because you're always on the search for someone better.

When people are asked why they are still single, many reply that they're still single against their wishes. Often they answer 'Because I haven't met the right man or woman.' But maybe, just maybe, God has sent you ten good men but you've been too afraid to get to know them better. You never know! It doesn't make sense to mourn missed chances in the past. It *does* make sense to make new choices in the future.

THE RIGHT ONE FOR SOMEONE ELSE

You can also long for the perfect partner because you aren't willing to deal with your own imperfections. Take Hannah, for example. Hannah (28) is a doctor, always looks good, and has an active social life. She's looking for a man who has a good job, dresses in expensive clothing, is athletic and, above all, good-looking. Her greatest wish is that he sails. She also expects him to have a fun social life and a strong faith. Finally, he should be comfortable in speaking in front of crowds and he should also be energetic. 'I just want someone who can handle me,' she tells her friends. Hannah has never been on a date.

It is often difficult, particularly for perfectionistic women, to find someone who meets all of their requirements. This is often because it is not possible for perfectionistic people to meet their *own* stringent requirements. Despite Hannah's job, social life and appearance, she is particularly insecure. Not many people are aware of that; you have to know Hannah well to be aware of that insecurity. But Hannah is always looking for ways to do things better and better, to have a more fulfilling social life, to lose five more pounds. She hopes that if her life can improve to a certain level, then 'the one' might come.

The question is why Hannah is even looking for 'the one'. Maybe an even more important question for Hannah to ask herself is 'Are you "the one" for someone else?' This a painful yet crucial question to ask yourself.

When I asked Hannah that question after a workshop, she looked visibly alarmed. 'Oops,' she said, looking thoughtfully into the distance. 'You know, I've never really thought about it. I hope to be ... But I know I am far from perfect.' Often people realize just what they're asking once they put themselves in the shoes of the person they're critiquing. Are you *always* fun and social? Are you *always* warm, charming and engaging? Are you a model Christian at all times and in all places, even when no one is watching? If your answer is 'yes' to these questions, then it's time for you to find a good therapist, because something is missing in your self-reflection. Is the answer 'no'? Good – you're honest. Now why are you searching for perfection in another person?

What Hannah wants in a man is perfection; mostly because she desperately wants to be perfect herself. What would be even more interesting for Hannah might be a man who isn't 'perfect' in the world's eyes – maybe with big ears or a crooked nose!

Hannah's challenge is to see beauty in imperfection. Only then will she be able to accept herself as she is: critical, demanding and ambitious. In one sense, there's nothing wrong with that. The positive side of those qualities can mean achieving great things here on earth. But more important character qualities are the ones that God continues to develop in us: grace, love, warmth and authenticity, qualities that are most visible in imperfect conditions. God looks at our heart and is concerned with our holiness, not our bank account or CV.

Henry (43) has another problem. He doesn't look at himself critically *enough*. According to Henry:

> I can't help that all of these women tell me 'no'. I really try but some people are just unlucky in love. Well, that's me. Something always gets in between me and love even although I'm a really good guy and have a lot to offer.

Now Henry really is a 'good guy' but I see why he's not in a relationship. It's not about his physical appearance, although he really could get his hair cut more often or wear clothes that fit him better. But the unattractive thing about Henry is his endless identity as a victim. Talk to Henry and you get a one-way complaining session.

Henry first came to my practice because of an anxiety disorder. He had panic attacks and was experiencing burnout from the continual fear and anxiety that dominated his life. But through that first session with him I learned that the source of Henry's anxiety was different from what he thought. 'I don't know if marriage is ever going to happen for me,' he said. 'And while I do really want a relationship, I also wonder what is going wrong.'

Guess what? Henry always asked women out whom he admired and looked up to but were much younger then him. 'Those are the women I really feel something for,' he said. 'But they don't want you!' I pointed out. 'But I don't find any of the others interesting.' 'Yes,' I countered, 'but the others are a better fit for you. Do you want something that's actually real?' That question proved difficult for Henry to answer. In the course of the conversation he had been able to take a more realistic look at himself, learning what kinds of women he actually fits well with; women with whom he could communicate on the same level. Now Henry finds much more enjoyment in dating, and his complaining is tapering off.

Many women complain about single men who are passive or not as 'quality' as married men. 'All the good men are taken!' cried Hannah when she learned about the dating courses I gave. 'I'll bet no real men come, just dorks.' 'There are some really nice men there,' I answered. 'The question is, whether you're prepared to see that they're there.'

Many women look at married men and think that they were equally mature when they were still single. But if you ask the men's wives you discover that nine out of ten had their own strange tendencies or dressed badly. I remember, for example, a friend who had been married ten years talking about her engagement: 'He always looked super nice,' she laughed:

And then we had a date and all of a sudden he was wearing this ugly shirt and weird baggy trousers. What happened? He had always gone shopping with his mother and sister and they chose his clothes. As long as he wore those, he looked good. But if he was dressing himself, he pulled the strangest combinations out of the wardrobe.

Now, appearance isn't everything, although that's often what we pay attention to on a date. Personal development is much more important. Most men – and women – I know would really like to grow further as a person, and preferably within an intimate relationship. Some, however, find this step difficult. Take Martin from the earlier example, married to Laura: 'I was always a bit shy,' he admitted. 'I also think that I had a low self-esteem. I didn't see what I had to offer a woman, and began to find it normal if they rejected me after a short time of dating, or even one date.'

Martin's uncertainty made him unattractive:

When I met Laura and she told me what she liked about me, that she appreciated me, I felt my confidence growing. I think that is when I really started to develop. I felt more like a man next to her. She called on me to protect her and to lead. I discovered that I could do that and wanted to. Looking back, it seems that before I met Laura I had been asleep, and she helped me to wake up.

Too many men I encounter seem asleep. They literally appear to be unable to see the women around them, or they make themselves invisible to women. It's no wonder so many woman are complaining of a lack of good men in the Church. Yes, there are statistically more women than men in the Church but there are some good men out there who remain silent. That's a shame, because I think there are many good men with potential who just need a kick in the backside! And often women aren't aware of how little they're opening up; how little they invite these men to ask them out; or how they fail simply to make contact.

Are you eager to meet 'the one'? More importantly, are you 'the one'?

GET TO KNOW YOURSELF

What I mean by this is: spend time reflecting by yourself, getting to know yourself. Take yourself out for coffee and think about what kind of company you make. Are you as fun as you're hoping someone else will be? Are you setting the bar as high for yourself as you do for others? Imagine that you're watching your own life on film. How would a partner fit into your schedule? When would you have time, energy or attention for another person? Look at the way you spend your money: how could your spending habits come across to your potential significant other? Consider the way you develop yourself: what topics can you bring to the table other than your work? Do you engage in activities you love, or are you waiting with all of that until you have found 'the one'?

Here's the thing about dating yourself: you may find you have a type, a list or a set of demands. You may even want to keep those. But in the end it comes back to Jesus' saying 'whatever you wish that others would do to you, do also to them, for this is the Law and the Prophets' (Matthew 7.12). How would he feel about your preferences? Would you be happy for someone to apply a similar list to you?

Your connection with others begins with your connection with God and your connection with yourself. Real connection also means seeing less beautiful sides of yourself, and is sometimes a painful process. Hannah must learn that she can be many things, even every now and then unfriendly or cranky, and that it's okay – nobody's perfect. Dating out of a connectedness with yourself makes the process much less complicated, actually. Once it's easier to be aware of how you feel around someone new and what it says about yourself and the other person, it's easier to distinguish good dates from bad ones. Good dates are the ones where you have a genuine heart-to-heart meeting; bad dates are the ones where it's not about you or the other person but about status, looks or other unimportant details.

In the short term this can be quite challenging. Don't despair! Taking up this challenge now prepares you for ones ahead, when you enter into a relationship where there is real intimacy.

THE SEARCH FOR BETTER

Here's another question to ask when taking yourself out for coffee. Take the criticism you've used on singles of the opposite sex, and apply it to yourself. Are you a woman who is annoyed with how little initiative men take? Are you convinced that men aren't trustworthy and are too indecisive and play games in dating? How encouraging are you yourself? Look in the mirror. If you were a man, would you want to date you? If the answer is no, what is the reason? Yes, sometimes men can be passive. But so many women are taking all of the imitative themselves, not giving men a chance.

This may also apply to men. Do you think women are too demanding or critical? Turn the question around. Don't stay in the role of victim, rather search for women you really like. If you're convinced they don't exist, take a good look around. Then, take the initiative. Don't wait until someone comes along but take a step towards a nice woman, even if you think she might turn you down.

'But there aren't any good men/women out there,' people say after taking one of my workshops. Really? Are you *sure*? On the whole earth there is not one person who is single and who you could like, even a little bit? Then I guess you're out of luck. Too bad that you'll spend your life alone. And how is it going for the man you broke up with because he doesn't have his masters degree when you do, and you insisted he didn't fit your standards? Oh, he's got a cute girlfriend who has a masters? Wow, you really do have bad luck. And what was wrong with that woman you ended a relationship with? Not pretty enough, that was it – yes, it would be very annoying to have to wake up each morning of your life next to someone who's not a model. Oh, she's married? To a successful businessman? Hmm.

The person who remains in a position of looking down on others will most likely end up lonely. In her book *Mr Good Enough*, mentioned in the previous chapter, Lori Gottlieb describes a type of woman who is always looking for a better man.[6] Sometimes these women are in relationships but they end them, thinking there is something better out there. Does your current boyfriend have an amazing job, and look good, but is his faith not as stable or important to him as you think it should be? That may be a deal breaker, or it may not, if he is genuinely growing in his faith. But on the other hand, there's a very good chance that you may find a boyfriend with a sincere and stable faith but who doesn't have an impressive job or handsome face. If you're always on the search for the more 'perfect package', you may find yourself alone.

'The problem is that no one goes "all-in" for me,' complained Pia (53). 'They always want a younger woman, a prettier woman, someone who hasn't been divorced.' 'And what are you looking for?' I asked, warily. 'For a suitable man!' 'In what age category, and where are you looking?'

> Oh, on the internet, for men my age or younger. Men who are older than 55 seem so old. And I don't want a widower, someone with the memory of a dead wife – ugh. And also someone without children. I don't have children of my own, so that would never work . . .

I looked at her in amazement. 'So you're allowed to set your standards but a man isn't allowed to have those same standards for you?' I asked to be certain. Pia nodded hesitantly. 'It does sound strange when you put it like that,' she admitted. 'But that's not what I mean.' 'What do you mean, then?' I asked cautiously. 'Oh, just a man who will go after me. Who is a little like me.' She sighed. 'But men just don't want me!' she cried, incensed. 'They just go for the 20- or 30-somethings!' (That may actually be true for some men, but they have problems of their own.)

In life in general, you reap what you sow. This is also true in dating. Are you picky? You may then encounter other choosy people and find yourself more rejected more often. If you consciously look at your choices, are you negative about men or fair in your critique of women? You'll get the same treatment. Make sure you think it over.

In some circles of women in the Church, it's fairly common to speak negatively about men. They're 'all wimps', 'totally lacking initiative', 'complete players' is most of the commentary. And maybe they're right. But if you keep hoping for a solid man, if you keep trusting that they exist, and keep looking, you're more likely to find one, and you'll go much further.

WHEN IT COMES TO SEXUALITY

Connecting to yourself is also connecting to your own sexuality. God created sex for connection to someone else; that is its design. I personally believe that God created sex for marriage between a man and woman. This is the boundary that my husband and I kept too, much to the surprise of the City Council official who married us in the usual Dutch traditional legal ceremony before the church service – a surprise she, in all her Dutch bluntness, didn't hide, much to the amusement of our guests, who knew us well. But what do you do with your sexuality when you're not in a relationship? And what do you do when you're in a relationship but not yet married? These are complicated questions, and I will not give you easy answers.

First of all, there are more ways to be sexual than having sex. Expressing your sexuality can also mean caring well for yourself and dressing in stylish clothes. For a woman it means showing that you're a woman, not through inappropriately low-cut tops and short skirts for example, but not hiding yourself away in oversized t-shirts and trousers either. If you're a man, show that you're a man. Don't hide yourself in clothing that communicates 'I'm not ready to be a responsible adult yet.' Develop your own style. Determine your own boundaries.

Your singleness is the time to define your sexual boundaries for future relationships. You can wait until you're in love but it's often much more difficult then. Of course, once you're in a relationship, you will need to discuss and agree on the boundaries for the physical side of your relationship, and how your sexuality will be expressed when you're together – more about that in Chapter 4. But even before that, in your single years, it is important to decide what boundaries you find acceptable in dating, engagement and marriage.

'Dating doesn't involve kissing,' I always reiterate at workshops and dating courses – and as I've mentioned in the introduction. Not because I'm so terribly prudish but more because physical contact so easily clouds those first, vulnerable stages of a relationship. The clearer you make the boundaries for yourself, the easier it will be to stick to them. And you'll also find that the clarity takes the pressure off. A date is so much more relaxed if you don't have to think about your breath quite so much, or your unshaven legs! You really have enough to think about on the first date.

Connecting to your sexuality also means that you 'own' your sexuality instead of it 'owning' you. You are the boss, so it won't end up being lust making the decisions, but it will consciously and intentionally be your brain instead. With you as boss, you won't need to work as hard to be as sexy or attractive. Of course flirting can sometimes play a role in dating, but within healthy boundaries.

HEALTHY BOUNDARIES

Where those healthy boundary lines are drawn is ultimately between you and God. But it can be liberating to put yourself in the other person's place. Do you really want to treat your date this way? What signals do you give, and what are you willing to receive? Often the boundary lines are crossed out of selfish motives.

'I just wanted to enjoy kissing someone,' said Lizzie, shrugging. 'And what did he think?' 'Um, yeah, but whatever, I don't care,' she admitted, knowing she wasn't giving the clearest signals.

In general, it's better to be too careful in the area of sexuality than to move too fast. Going back to an earlier boundary is far more difficult than moving towards the next one. If you've already petted and caressed each other, than it's going to be tricky to feel satisfied with just kissing. At the same time, kissing will probably give you less regret than fondling or intercourse.

Lust is something that betrays us by surprising our judgement, making us less able to think about the consequences of our actions. The first six weeks of a new relationship may feel like the perfect time to do anything and everything, especially on a physical and sexual level. And maybe you're both most likely to agree to more than you should. But after one week, six weeks or eight, that first infatuation is gone and if you're left with someone with whom you actually don't have that much in common, then you have a problem. Maybe you've had a fun six weeks but the reality that it's superficial is hitting you hard. Detaching yourself from someone you have gone a long way with physically is much more difficult than from someone with whom you've just shared a kiss.

God created us as sexual beings, and we needn't hide that. The fact that you 'shouldn't' have sex as a single person doesn't mean that you can't enjoy people of the opposite sex. But think in terms of the future; often too much pleasure too soon creates too much regret. Setting healthy boundaries when you're single helps you set healthy boundaries later. Monogamy within marriage begins with sexual purity as a single. The more purely you deal with sex as a single person, the easier it will be to do this in your marriage and be faithful to your partner for the rest of your life.

It's the same for masturbation; we can't label it good or bad. It may even help you not to be so obsessed with sex. But be careful; this is an area that can easily become dangerous. Dangerous for your soul, dangerous for your personal development. So find help! Don't stay isolated in your struggle but look for a good therapist or support group.[7] There are some great resources that can help if you're struggling with porn or masturbation, and we've listed these at the back of the book. Enjoyable sexuality within marriage begins with single people who are striving for healthy sexuality that is neither too strict nor too uncontrolled.

The beauty of dealing with sexuality in a pure, refined way is that you can use it in a positive way throughout the dating process. If you're aware of your masculinity or femininity, you can use that awareness when you date. Flirting is ultimately an expression of sexual energy.

Some singles have just a bit too much sexual energy, and allow it to influence them. Just as Ben (32) says 'I flirt too much. I know I do it, but I just love women. Now I think it's time to rein in my sexual energy a bit.' By his own admission, Ben often attracts the 'wrong' types. 'Women who want more right away. Women who give me attention, compliments,' he sighed. 'I do the same. I give them compliments and attention and presents. But I'm looking for a woman who challenges me, someone who is my equal. Someone who dares to say every now and then, "Don't be ridiculous, Ben!"'

Other singles are too disconnected from their sexuality. Often they're not aware of how they're perceived by others, they're not dressing attractively or they're neglecting themselves a bit. Sometimes the way they dress even makes them a bit invisible. Sexuality gives colour and sparkle to life, even to life as a single person.

Live with both hands open: one to receive and the other to take a hold of healthy boundaries. Instead of living like a wallflower, ladies, buy a sexy dress and let your hair loose. Guys, go ahead and tell that joke you find so funny, and polish your shoes. But don't be tempted to use selfish flirting. There are lots of reasons why God says that sex is only for within marriage. In the world's eyes you can have sex with anyone but that won't involve the pure and true intimacy He wants us to have. Boundaries are not intended to spoil your fun but to protect that intimacy until it's time for it to awaken. And intimacy is exactly what you'll need in the long term to keep a relationship interesting.

BEING COMFORTABLE IN YOUR OWN SKIN

Finally, it is important to invest in yourself as much as you invest in good friendships. Dating is much more enjoyable if you feel comfortable in your own skin. Connecting with yourself can be a good remedy for loneliness. Be careful that you don't begin to date out of a deep sense of loneliness. Put even more strongly: you can feel lonely from time to time *even if you're married*, or maybe especially when you're married and the one you love and share your life with does not understand you, or does not seem to listen; when you try to connect but the person with whom you share a house is just not 'there', not present with you emotionally.

Henry, mentioned earlier in this chapter, was typical of a single person who wasn't comfortable being fully himself while he was single. Interestingly enough, this was also reflected in his own home, which was cold and empty. 'I can buy furniture,'

Henry replied when I asked 'But what would I do if I met a woman tomorrow who had a different taste?' 'If you met a woman tomorrow, and ended up marrying her, then you could take the furniture you've just bought and donate it to a good cause,' I answered. 'But live for today! Make choices that are important for you in the here and now, and make sure you feel at home in your own house.'

If you're comfortable with who you are, and are not putting life on hold until you meet someone, then you're already investing in your future relationship. If you're able to discover now what is important to you, you have less of a chance of adapting too much to your partner and losing yourself in the relationship – and therefore losing the relationship. To put it clearly: try to enjoy your singleness to the point that when you meet that wonderful person, you can say: 'Now I've got to give up my single status, fun as it was, but life with you is even better!'

LONGING FOR A RELATIONSHIP: HEALTHY DISCONTENT

Your longing for a relationship is a good and understandable longing. It's this very desire that can lead to meaningful action in this area of your life. If you're in search of a partner, it is good to start with yourself.

Meg Jay, an American psychotherapist and author of *The Defining Decade*, emphasizes just how important it is for 20-somethings to learn about themselves as they pursue relationships at home or at work: 'We may hear that thirty is the new twenty, but – recession or not – when it comes to work and love and the brain and the body, forty is definitely not the new thirty.'[8] Too many 20-somethings are asleep, unconsciously letting life drift by. If you're in this age group and want to get married, take the initiative and work on your personal growth. Don't wait until you're 40. And don't think you're alone: 'I have yet to meet a twenty-something who doesn't want to get married or at least find a committed relationship.'[9]

Sometimes during this process of focusing on yourself, it's better for some singles to put dating on hold for a period of time. Take Karl (32), who concluded after attending my course that:

> Actually, for me the right thing is to take a year's break from dating. I've had a steady stream of girlfriends since I was fifteen. It's time to be alone for a while, to discover my own needs and motives, to seek and know God, and to discover my own self-worth without a girlfriend.

For most people, it starts here. Dating is much more interesting and enjoyable when paired with self-reflection. When you have an open, inquisitive attitude towards yourself, you often discover hidden treasure you haven't seen before. Then dating becomes a rich opportunity for self-knowledge. But it's about more than just connecting to yourself. In the following chapter we'll take a look at how we connect to the people around us.

QUESTIONS FOR FURTHER REFLECTION

- What have you learned from your previous relationships? What obstacles or stumbling blocks might there be in your dating life?
- What are your lifestyle habits, and how do you fill your schedule?
- How many new people do you come across who are also single?
- Do you have a 'type'?

- What's your experience with dating websites?
- Is there a stigma connected to dating websites? Is it strange to say that you 'met someone on the internet'?
- What are your boundaries when it comes to sex and dating, or engagement and beyond?

ASSIGNMENTS

- Write out your relationship-history timeline.
- Meet five new single people per week.
- Make a list – as long as you want – of all of the qualities you're looking for in a partner. Next, choose the five most important qualities on the list.
- Take yourself on a date. You don't need to go to a café or restaurant, although you may choose to. You can also just take time in the comfort of your own home to reflect on the questions that stood out for you in this chapter. Either way, the main focus is this: to what extent you are 'the one' for someone else, and how might that reality shape your future dating experiences?

Leabharlanna Poiblí Chathair Bhaile Átha Cliath
Dublin City Public Libraries

3 Connecting to a community

The best foundation for dating is laid by connecting to the people around you, your community. I call this 'dating with a team'. I came across this concept of a 'team' for the first time in Henry Cloud's book, *How to Get a Date Worth Keeping*.[1] When first encountering Cloud's phrase 'your team', I imagined hosting a big gathering, inviting everyone I planned on including in my dating life, which seemed a bit complicated. But Cloud's idea, put into practice, is better than I had expected. The truth of the matter is this: if you're single, you can use a good team of people around you. In this chapter I explain how connecting to a team enriches your dating life.

YOU DON'T HAVE TO DO IT ALONE

Sure, you might find yourself in a pub or restaurant alone with your date. It's very likely that you haven't opted to take a chaperone. You may go on a date alone but you don't have to do the whole process of dating alone. In the American 'courtship movement', the well-intentioned people who are a bit 'anti-dating' (see Chapter 1), dating in a group is promoted as an alternative to one-to-one dating.

From the courtship perspective, meeting someone in the company of your team, or at least part of your team, is an ideal scenario – except that I don't believe this is really the most help-ful way to get to know somebody. Of course, sometimes you can get to know somebody in a group setting with whom you later meet up for a one-to-one conversation. That's great. But dating is exactly about the tension that exists with the other person when you meet one-to-one. You need to learn how to accept the possibility that you might become hurt, or hurt another person. Your team is no buffer against that.

In 'dating with a team' it's important to remember that you're not alone. You don't have to decide on your own if this was a date worth repeating, but can invite people into the events of your dating life. Even if you are hurt or want to end the relationship, your team can be there for comfort or wise advice. This helps especially if they've been involved since the very beginning.

When I began to dare to date myself, I gave Cloud's *How to Get a Date Worth Keeping* to a girlfriend and my sister. They were the first to understand why this book had touched, helped and changed me. Because of the importance of their insight into both my life and the new relationship with the man who is now my husband, the same sister and friend were both witnesses at my wedding. For me, the process of daring to date in a meaningful way began when I gave Cloud's book as a gift to people within my community. I wanted to give up the fight, to surrender to my pervasive feeling of sadness about remaining single.

Admitting my sadness didn't feel good at the time but in hindsight was the important first step towards a different attitude. With this honesty I was finally free to admit: 'I'm single and don't like it.' From there I was able to make some changes. Eventually, being honest with others about how I felt was liberating.

The friend who read Cloud's book and had listened to the stories of all of my dating experiences also describes that moment as life-changing for her. As a married woman she wanted to acknowledge my feelings but also try to help me face the reality of the difficulties of marriage. Marriage wasn't always fantastic and she told me so: 'It is also hard work. And the work isn't always fun.' I felt as if she was dismissing my pain, and this made me angry. 'So are you saying I have nothing to complain about? That makes me feel like I'm not allowed to be sad about being single!' I added: 'I don't care if marriage is hard work! Bring it on! I'm ready.'

Now that I am married, I have a better understanding of what she meant by the idea that marriage isn't everything, designed to end all your unhappiness or loneliness. Often it happens this way: you're single for years, and finally end up in a long-term, committed relationship. You briefly enjoy how much nicer it is to be in a relationship rather than being alone, only to find yourself then focusing on what you're missing in the new relationship that you'd enjoyed when you were single. That's just human nature.

So when your friend laments that 'Marriage is isn't everything', then she is also probably forgetting how miserable she sometimes felt when she was single. But I still stand by the opinion that I'd rather be in a relationship than not, including all of the extra investments and sacrifices a relationship requires.

Another positive side of having a lot of girlfriends who were in a relationship or married was that they kept my ideals and expectations realistic. I was never able to have sweeping, romantic fantasies about marriage. My work as a relational therapist never permitted it, and neither did my healthy encounters with reality through the lives of married friends or friends with families.

I've always been very lucky to have a community of friends and family who shared their lives with me. My sister's door was always open, and as a single I found relief from time to time in the rhythms and structure of my sister's family life. It kept me grounded.

Sometimes as a single person you miss the presence of children in your life. Through experiencing life with another family, you can sometimes compensate for this a bit by cuddling and playing with the children of friends or family. Or if you're single with children, you can let your children be hugged by others while you're resting at your friend's or family's place. You don't need to do life alone, even if you're single. Sometimes single people choose to have housemates and really enjoy them. Others choose to get involved in organizations or classes, or even small groups at church.

It is in the context of these relationships, your community, that you can share your dating life. But not just your dating life. There is so much more to discuss. Sometimes I find it strange that many singles' conversations are mostly complaints about their dating lives. It can be good to vent. If you need to just 'get it out', venting can help. But there is so much more to talk about.

LET YOUR FRIENDS LOVE YOU

'No man is an island', wrote the poet John Donne. Just as no one is an island, no one grows or flourishes without people around. A shocking study done by the Austrian psychoanalyst René Spitz in 1945 revealed the reason behind infant mortality rates in Russian orphanages.[2] One group of babies were placed in orphanages where they received enough nutrition and were cared for using strict hygienic procedures. The other group of babies were placed back with their mothers who were in prison. Spitz found that the babies who were with their mothers did better on every level, although circumstances in terms of feeding and hygiene were much worse.

In the orphanages, workers wearing latex gloves were washing the babies, swaddling them and then putting them down in such a way that the babies could not touch each other. One by one the children began to die. The staff were flummoxed until they discovered what it was that the children were missing: being picked up and cuddled, and being touched. Children need to feel that you are there and that you love them. Words are not enough. Man doesn't live by food and cleanliness alone. We all must be embraced and touched in order to develop as healthy people.

If the lack of touch literally means death for infants, what does it mean for adults? So many single people, especially men, are never embraced. For me as a single, my switch to a more non-traditional church was a relief. Every Sunday I was really *hugged*, properly, by people near and dear to me in the church. I wish every single could experience those hugs. Even as adults, we all need to be loved physically in order to flourish as we were meant to. We need both to give and to receive appropriate physical affection.

Don't date in order to feel loved. You should receive love first and foremost from your team, your friends and family. Dating may result in a lot of disappointments and, if you're taking the risks you should, rejections. As Cloud himself states: 'I want you to get rejected as much as possible! This way I know that you're at least trying.'[3]

Look for love in your immediate circle from people you've known and trusted for years, people who have seen you through both high and low moments in your life. These people can honestly tell you what they think about your current situation.

If you meet someone for coffee who tells you after one date 'I don't think I see anything happening here', this will feel a lot less like rejection when you are surrounded by people who have known you for years – the kind of people with whom you can be grumpy as you're sitting at their kitchen table, because of a hangover or just because it wasn't your day. Make sure you have people in your life, friends or family, with whom you feel at home and who love you. Make sure you aren't getting your sense of self-worth from your dating experiences but from people with whom you have history, people who know you well.

Dating with a supportive team allows you to turn again and again to the people who know and see you exactly as you are. I implicitly trusted my friends and my sister, namely for their love and support. They would say things like 'You can do it. He's an idiot, and we love you.' I've also known men who do this for each other, giving strong encouragement every now and then: 'Come on, man, go for it. Let her know what you think of her. Even if you don't know if she's interested.'

THE INVERTED FUNNEL

Daring to date means that you need your community, people who can encourage you, help keep you motivated. Dating can be an ongoing struggle, not often simply an easy or fun endeavour. There is always an element of tension and a very real risk of rejection. The tendency, therefore, can be to give up. It's natural to give yourself the time you need to recover after a series of dates that seemed promising but didn't evolve further, or after a short- or long-term relationship that has ended. It can even be good sometimes to refrain from dating to give yourself time to lick your wounds, so to speak. At the same time, it is also important to give your team permission to tell you: 'Come on, it's time to move on.' Give them the permission to ask about your dating life. This is something you should ask your team very directly. Bring it up yourself in conversation; most people don't dare ask you unless you give them permission.

My friend Rebecca has the same perspective. We have a mutual friend in Hannah from the previous chapter, and Rebecca confided in me that she found it difficult to challenge Hannah about her approach to dating. She was afraid that it would come across wrongly but explained her concerns to me.

> Hannah is such a perfectionist! I think that she's too demanding but I'm afraid to tell her. The worst is, when she talks about what kind of man she's looking for – handsome, tall, well dressed, articulate and everything, the whole song and dance – I'm almost ashamed of my husband. Because then I think: 'He doesn't have all of those qualities. But I'm so completely happy with him! He is sweet and gentle but, for example, is not such a great public speaker.' I get it. Before I met David I wanted the kind of man she described, and it took me a little while to accept the difference, but now I wouldn't have it any other way.

It touched me to think how the demands or wishes on Hannah's list made Rebecca feel that her own husband had possible shortcomings. How many friends did I unwittingly hurt by enumerating my own (stupid) wish list? But above all, how difficult did I make it for myself with my own perfectionistic tendencies? When I was single I always responded to the comment

'You're too picky' with 'And why not? Why shouldn't I be choosy about the person I will share the rest of my life with? In my opinion, you can't be picky enough.' It sounded convincing enough, even to me. Now I understand that this was only half of the story. The other half of the story was that I was often so afraid of being hurt or rejected that I kept a careful distance from eligible men.

Many people use an 'inverted funnel' approach when dating. By this I mean that they see too little potential in the people around them, limiting themselves to a very few, carefully chosen dates. And then they're often too critical, keeping the entrance criteria far too narrow. This is just like attempting to pour water into the wrong end – the narrowest part of the funnel. Dating with such narrow entry requirements can provoke the same kind of frustration and disappointment.

If you're dating, turn the funnel around so that the wide end faces up and the narrow end faces down. Henry Cloud says 'Go out with almost anyone once, and maybe again.'[4] You will then have more opportunities to go out with more people, and you may grow to like someone more over time. Eventually, dating a range of people may lead to meeting one person you are more serious about.

It is very important to be objective enough when dating turns into 'serious dating'. The one big difference is this: once you begin to date somebody in earnest, you begin to look at him or her through the lens of the heart, and feelings can get in the way of clear thinking.

If you get to know the heart of the other person, really get to know that person, and then hit on large obstacles that you cannot overcome, it's time to say goodbye to the relationship.

However, that shouldn't simply be only a logical decision, and definitely not based just on physical attractiveness. Once you're completely in love with somebody with whom you're in a relationship, the risk is that it becomes increasingly difficult to be objective and see the flaws in the relationship. You simply stop filtering. And before you know it, you find yourself months or even years into a relationship of which everybody in your surroundings thinks: 'They're not right for each other.'

Many marriages have begun with fairly compelling feelings of infatuation but with a serious lack of critical and thoughtful evaluation of what similarities really exist between them – such as convictions, values and goals. Sooner or later the moment comes when you have to face those things. Too often that's when people sigh, saying 'If only we'd been honest about this from the beginning.'

This is where your team becomes even more important. They're your brain for that first phase of dating. When you first meet someone and become infatuated, you lose your ability to think rationally. It's difficult to see what's really best and what really suits you in the long term. Your brain is in a drugged state. An infatuated brain can be compared with a brain that's under the influence of cocaine.[5] You experience an intense and addictive high and tend to rely purely on feelings.

In this first phase you'll also find yourself responding in black and white terms. No spark? The strategy is often an immediate 'not for me' and escape. Find someone very interesting? Then people may answer too quickly with a 'yes' and jump right into a serious relationship. Neither response is ideal. Ask your team for help. At this point in the relationship, your team can often see things more clearly than you can.

A KICK IN THE BEHIND

Sometimes as a single person you need to be confronted, challenged. Sometimes you need even more than that. A friend of mine always tells about how his team often functioned as a 'kick in the behind'. Their advice was 'Go for it', sometimes even 'Don't take "no" for an answer. Ask her one more time.' That may sound a little crazy, but in dating you can easily become disillusioned. Dating can be extremely daunting if you've been turned down for the umpteenth time.

After the conclusion of a workshop, Vincent (42) confided in me: 'I'll ask a woman out if I'm 98 or 99 per cent certain she'll say yes. And I'm not the only man who does that!' What a shame for Vincent and his single friends. Singleness is the burden they bear, but with this strategy, very little will change.

A friend of mine said to me that men in particular can use this kind of thinking, and explained:

> Rejection is not fun, so the safest option is to withdraw. If you don't ask her, she can't tell you 'no'. It's precisely in these sort of situations that you need friends who encourage you to go for it anyway. Maybe you end up feeling a bit downhearted but that is always better than never having tried in the first place.

Someone within a healthy community can't hang on to self-pity as easily as someone without community. Eventually you will hear your loved ones say to you: 'I know, I know. You're sad, frustrated, disappointed. I love you but it's time to stop moaning and do something.'

Sometimes people who are single lack healthy feedback. They keep the complaining to themselves, out of fear of conflict or vulnerability, and avoid saying what they really feel to their loving friends or family. This is disadvantageous, because what they might really need hear is this: 'Your moaning and groaning doesn't bring you any closer to a relationship. Feel free to complain, but it doesn't help.'

Sometimes the only thing you need is a good kick in the behind. During adolescence you probably got this from your father or mother, if your relationship with them was healthy, or you got it from your peers. But too often single people who live alone receive little or no correction or feedback from others. As soon as Vincent began to date with the encouragement of his team, he became a lot happier. Now he's is married to someone he wanted to marry for a very long time. 'She asked me out on the first date,' he grinned, 'but I was very quick to arrange all of the following dates myself!' Vincent's wife winked at me: 'After the first date, I only needed to say "yes" to his invitations.'

CHALLENGE, EVALUATE AND MIRROR YOUR DATES WITH YOUR TEAM

Let's say you begin to date and find yourself making some stupid decisions. On the one hand there are people who say 'no' too often in response to dates or ask for too few dates; on the other hand, you have those people who are too quick to jump into a relationship. If you tend to bounce around from one relationship to another or notice that you're not single for very long between relationships, then it can be very good to give your team permission – to quote Henry Cloud – to 'tie you to a tree'. He explains: '"Tie me to a tree" means you empower a team of people to confront you and prevent you from falling into self-destructive behaviors.'[6]

This was what Leeann (30) needed. She admitted at our coaching session that she wasn't often single for long: 'In one way or another I end up with a guy, and after several months, I begin wondering, "Why don't you ever just get on with things?"' Leeann doesn't notice the man's lack of initiative in the beginning, but as the months continue she is increasingly aware that it wasn't there from the start. She's simply in love and goes for 'it'; and 'it' becomes a relationship. She told us that in retrospect she sees that her habit of always taking the initiative has caused an imbalance in her relationships.

Leeann is a nice person – active, enterprising, open and sweet. She's the kind of woman men find attractive. It's not that she's exceptionally beautiful but she has a very open and inviting manner. This is also her pitfall. She's able to connect with men so easily that she's soon smitten. One conversation leads to a date, one date becomes a second date, and before she knows it, the dates have evolved into a relationship in which she finds herself attached. Without even realizing, Leeann is often the one who calls, who asks for a second date, who says 'I'd like to see you more often.'

Even though Leeann seems to get into a relationship easily, often the relationship begins to wear on her after a while. 'I'm always the one calling', she said. 'He never calls. He never makes plans for the weekend. I always come up with the ideas.' 'But, my dear Leeann, you're doing this to yourself!' I told her one day. We were sitting on a terrace, discussing her umpteenth disappointing relationship: 'You're setting the tone in the beginning. *You* call. *You* plan the weekend. What did you think would happen? The man finds himself in a nice, easy position. Why *should* he take the initiative?'

Leeann sighed: 'But what should I do? If I do nothing, nothing happens.' It's quite possible that Leann is on to something. When I was interviewed about this subject, the interviewer told me afterwards: 'I don't know if I'd be married if my wife hadn't taken the initiative, you know?' And I know more than one man who was happily immersed in his own life when a woman came along and said: 'Hey, let's go out for a drink.'

Who takes the initiative first isn't so important, as your team may remind you. People ask all the time whether the man or the woman is supposed to take the initiative. For many women, the role of waiting is often a little difficult, especially if there aren't many men in their professional or personal spheres. In that case, taking the initiative is tempting. But opinions differ. Some people think that it's perfectly fine if a woman takes the initiative. Others are convinced that the initiative is up to men. In my opinion, there is nothing wrong if a woman would like to initiate the first date, as long as that initiative doesn't remain one-sided. It's important for a woman to be inviting, to be open to the initiative from a man. Men often talk about women who are 'closed' or unapproachable.

If after several dates you're still the only one asking, you've got to ask yourself what's going on. From her past dating experiences, Leeann learned to step back a little and allow the men she was dating to take more action. It soon became clear to her that the men who didn't take the initiative just weren't that interested or had some personal growth to do, and she learned to let them go.

Ultimately, it is two people who have to decide to fight for a relationship. If one doesn't participate, then there is no relationship. It's the same with dating. Taking the initiative, for men and women alike, is good. But if you're continually the only one working at it, then you don't really have a relationship. Then the best thing to do is turn around and walk away.

However, if you conclude that someone isn't interested enough in you, it's useful to reflect on what the other person might be thinking or experiencing. Often she or he is actually taking steps and actions towards you but it's difficult for you to see that. Your team can help you gain insight into this. The best thing you can do is let them ask about your experiences. How was your date? What did you notice about yourself? Were you at ease? Could you be yourself? How was the other person? How did you feel around them: safe or wary? And where could that sense come from?

When Hannah from the previous chapter asked her team at church to observe how she was around men, to her horror she found that they thought she seemed unavailable. 'You look arrogant,' they said. 'You don't have an inviting attitude. You look at the ground, you don't make eye contact.' This feedback wasn't easy to hear but she knew and trusted the people giving it. Above all, it helped her see how she really behaved to the men around her. What she already suspected was true: she wasn't available enough.

'I didn't want to believe it,' Hannah told me:

> I thought they were crazy. Am I not friendly? Don't I do my best? I was terrified to ask for their observations, but when my friend Rebecca explained that I exuded an 'I'm fine, I don't need you' attitude, I knew immediately what she meant.

Hannah blushed. 'Embarrassing, huh? *That's* how I come across? Especially when I like a guy – the thought just makes me shudder.'

'Look,' Rebecca told me, responding to Hannah's earlier comment, 'now it's finally getting interesting. Now we can actually have a conversation about her singleness rather than Hannah's long monologues and me giving sympathetic nods.' Rebecca's eyes began to glisten: 'And I can share my thoughts! It's really fun, actually,' she said, grinning. And then, more softly:

> I really care about Hannah and don't think it's her own fault that she's single, but there are things that we can change about ourselves for the better. And I love that now she's thinking things through with me rather than just feeling as powerless as she did.

What kind of impression do *you* give? This is an important question for your team. Is their feedback about how you come across actually what you want to exude? You may find dating really scary but do you really have to appear stiff and unnatural to your dates? Or have you chosen to face your fear and smile anyway at that man or woman you like? Who knows what might happen? And the more often you practise, the more normal it seems and the easier it becomes.

Ask your team what your pitfalls are in dating. Do you take too much initiative or not enough? Do you avoid eye contact? Or do you jump from one relationship to the next? Look at where your possibilities lie. It's good that you're taking the initiative but maybe if you're a woman you can take a bit less or be a bit more subtle. Great that you're taking the initiative as a man but are you trying to win the heart of everyone you date or are you also careful with the heart of the woman in question? And if you're shy, it's good that you're protective of your heart and not giving it away too freely, but are you ever getting out of your comfort zone? Are you too protective of yourself? You're made of tough fibre, you know. Your heart can take a little beating, especially if you have your team as a safety net.

In the next chapter I elaborate on how you can evaluate a date, including an evaluation tool. Here is a good place to involve your team. Let yourself be confronted! Allow them to mirror and help you to evaluate. This way, dating becomes much more informative, helping you to learn and grow with each experience.

DEFINING BOUNDARIES WITH YOUR TEAM

Another area where your team can play an important role is in helping you define your boundaries. When you begin dating, have a conversation with your team about what your sexual boundaries are. I believe in dating inside very clear boundaries. Physical contact creates a strong bond, whether you like it or not. In the film *Vanilla Sky*, Cameron Diaz's character sagely remarks 'Don't you know if you sleep with someone, your body makes a promise whether you do or not?'[7] It's the same with kissing. Intimate physical contact is a promise of more. Don't promise more if you don't intend to keep the promise in the future.

There are very good reasons for waiting until marriage to have sex. The reasons aren't spelled out in the Bible, at least not in so many words. But our blueprint for life is to love and follow God and the Bible is clear that sex is for within marriage, even if God doesn't spend ages explicitly going into the reasons for his design. Tim Keller does an excellent job explaining this theologically in his book *The Meaning of Marriage*.[8]

But what is at least as important for me as a psychologist and mental health professional is that there are good biological and psychological reasons to wait with sex too. As much impact as a kiss can have, heavy caressing or having sex creates even more impact. They work as bonding agents, as they were created to. Biologically, we know that there are all kinds of chemicals released in your brain when you have sex with someone. These are chemicals that serve to make you feel happy, relaxed and connected to your partner. But if you have sex with someone you don't know very well, these same chemicals serve to make you feel more fearful and insecure afterwards.

It is actually quite something to give in to lust, rather than using self-control, with God's help, to leave sex until marriage. Lust has real consequences. 'One-night stands just made my loneliness worse,' my non-believing friend admitted to me, 'so I stopped having them.' What we're often doing is bonding our bodies to someone before we've bonded our hearts to them, which is a shame. Not only is it a draining, empty experience, it also becomes difficult to open up to somebody emotionally who you've already been open with physically.

If you choose to outline your sexual boundaries to your team, you're also giving them permission to talk to you about what's happening within your relationships, to check in with you and make sure you're staying within your set limits. This means that they're also allowed to be challenging and confront you when you're not keeping to those limits. The good news is that this will mean there's a greater chance that you are taking your time to really get to know someone; and that you're not complicating the process by having sex with someone and making it more difficult for yourself to let go if you realize you don't want to take the relationship any further.

You can also discuss with your team where your boundaries are when it comes to giving out personal information. Mary had the tendency to share too much if she had a date with somebody she really liked. She also felt compelled to tell the man in question all of her faults. 'Really,' she said, 'maybe you won't believe me now, but I told him everything. And I mean *everything*.'

Mary then told me about the third date she had gone on with someone:

> The first two were fun and comfortable, and so of course I knew, *this is him*. The man I'm going to marry has arrived. I had even mentally planned the wedding. All he needed to do was ask. And so I thought 'Total openness, Mary, total openness. He had a right to know who he was going to marry. Can you imagine?

She looked at me intently. 'The *third* date.' She laughed and continued her story. 'So I told him, "You really should know that I can be very gloomy sometimes. Actually, a bit depressed. It runs in our family; my aunt is also depressive."' She made a face at me and cried: 'And that's not even true! Sure, I can be a bit pessimistic or gloomy but it doesn't mean I'm depressed.' She could laugh about it now. 'The poor guy! He became pale and didn't say anything. We didn't go out again, and all because I gave him the wrong idea.'

A reminder that it's not wise to pour your heart out to someone immediately is the kind of wisdom your team brings into your life. A date is a date and you've got a long way to go before you're married. You can talk about everything later, once you're sure you want to continue your relationship with this person. In fact you've got to have those conversations – but later! For now, there is no way to know after three dates whether you're going to marry this person. Don't let married people tell you this can happen. People tend to tell their love story through rose-tinted glasses, and the story tends to become 'rosier' with each passing year. Research shows that this is actually a thing: the story of 'how we met' sounds a bit more successful with each year that goes by. That's just how our brains work. We tend to polish good memories but forget the difficult ones.

THE CHURCH'S ROLE

Because we are each other's 'brothers and sisters', we are given stewardship over each other. This is one of the reasons why I find 'dating with your team' such a beautiful idea. Often people who are married within my community ask me 'What can I do to help single people find partners?' Exactly this: you can be on someone's team; you can coach, critique, give feedback and encourage. In fact you're extremely important!

The beauty about this arrangement is that you as a single person have control over who's involved in your dating life and who isn't. This prevents you from falling prey to poorly informed advice such as: 'Love will find you when you least expect it' or 'It will just happen.' Such advice can be well-intentioned and meant as encouraging but it's not something you want to hear. If you have control over the people who give you feedback, and how these conversations take place, it might save you from a few frustrating experiences.

Timothy Keller is the head pastor of Redeemer Presbyterian Church in New York City, a church with one of the highest numbers of single attenders worldwide. One of his best-known books, *The Meaning of Marriage*, is – of course – about marriage. However, in this book Keller also addresses the single person. One of his theories is that the sharply rising number of single people may be due to the disconnected communities in which we find ourselves. We no longer live in close-knit communities, says Keller, and therefore experience less pressure to marry. The fear of commitment is a long-standing human fear. But the healthy pressure of a community can be a good antidote to it. This pressure for singles is often lacking in large cities and churches.[9]

This is familiar in the churches I've been part of. It's fair to say that in the big cities within the Western – and non-Western – world, singleness is normal: over 50 per cent of Londoners, Parisians and the inhabitants of New York's Manhattan have a one-person household. For those of us who are single, that number is reassuring and a part of the reason why some of us choose to live in cities. But if you wish to get married one day, make sure you don't grow too comfortable in that majority position, Keller says. It's exactly this situation that makes a community so important.

Historically, Jewish communities often had a matchmaker – someone who was often quite curious and nosy but liked to look single community members in the eye and try to pick the best match for them. To our modern minds that seems a little *too* involved but I wonder what would happen if we were to have matchmakers in big cities.[10] What would change?

Many couples I know have met through some kind of intentional meeting arranged by someone else. It doesn't have to be a blatant set-up. It might be a casual mention in a conversation: 'Do you know so-and-so? Do you find them interesting?' Or two people meet each other at a party, find themselves on the same committee or sit at the same table at a wedding. It's all right if it doesn't end up being something, but a complete lack of intentionality pretty much guarantees failure.

The Church also is and should be working towards enabling healthier and more lasting relationships, no matter what the relationship status. Churches can encourage singles to be dating but also help them figure out how to do single life well, as much as they can help married couples do married life well, parenting well or even divorcing well. I think the Church can and should play a much bigger role when it comes to these issues and how to support those facing them.[11]

EXPANDING YOUR TEAM: CONSIDER COUNSELLING

For a long time I've emphasized that every single person above 25 should experience counselling. Back when I was 25, of course (in my arrogance), I didn't go to counselling – I was already a therapist myself. I had a few conversations with a student psychologist but this didn't make me much wiser. I finally found a good counsellor when I became 30. This experience has helped me make great strides in my own process of growth and has been a personal investment that I can recommend to anyone.

In fact counselling is a professional extension of your team. Of course, a coach or mentor can be very helpful, but a trained therapist or counsellor simply has more knowledge when it comes to issues that can affect single people, such as anxiety, and how to understand and handle them well.

When do you need counselling? Generally speaking, counselling can help if you're having difficulty overcoming the problems you're facing. If you're experiencing your singleness as challenging or if, in the course of a conversation with your team, you come across an issue that is very difficult to solve, then it can be really good to meet a few times with a professional to help guide you through to some greater understanding and ways forward.

Many singles wrestle with some form of fear. Even if you think you know what's causing it, it can be enormously helpful to meet with someone one-to-one and take a look at why you're feeling fear and at what might be done to improve things. At one point in my practice I was counselling Alice (39). She noticed that she was afraid to speak to men because of her hypersensitivity to her ears. She found them too protruding. She was so obsessive about her ears that she had convinced herself that men took one look at her ears and walked away. In her perspective, her ears were elephant-sized.

Just like Alice, many of the fears that keep people from dating are unrealistic and exaggerated. This is more easily recognizable in others than in yourself. Because of this, it's very helpful to determine what your fears might be when it comes to dating, and to talk over those fears. If your team notices this, it's wise to allow someone to help you.

Through counselling, Alice learned that even she, large ears and all, might be attractive to men. After about eight appointments, she got up the courage to begin dating, and six months later met the man she eventually married. Together they have a beautiful daughter. For Alice, the investment of eight appointments, four months of counselling and a few hundred euros was completely worth it. 'I waited a long time to ask for help,' she told me later, 'but I'm so happy I did. I wish I had taken that step earlier.'

For other people, of course, there may be entrenched issues that are affecting their dating life. They may have had very negative past experiences of relationships or the opposite sex, and counselling can help bring healing to these.

The lesson is this: sometimes it pays to expand your team to include professionals. It can be true for other things in your life as well. For example, if you have one wall in your home to paint, you can easily do this small job yourself. But if it comes to remodelling the whole bathroom, you hire a professional. Sometimes it's better to ask someone who has the knowledge and experience to do the work for you or with you.

QUESTIONS FOR FURTHER REFLECTION

- Do you already have a team, consciously or unconsciously? If yes, what kinds of people are on your team, and is it complete? If not, why not?
- Do you sometimes find dating difficult? What can your team do to help you continue?
- What are the topics your team could best challenge or confront you about? And for which ones do you need encouragement?

ASSIGNMENTS

- Put your team together. Ask friends, family members, a coach, a mentor or a therapist to walk alongside you in dating.
- Ask each member of your team the following:
  - o Why am I still single?
  - o What can I do about this?
  - o What do I/can I expect from you as a member of my team?
- Try to meet five new single people per week and evaluate your interactions with your team.

4 Connecting to the other person

If the previous chapters have had their intended effect, it is my hope that your perspective of dating has changed for the better. And if you've been able to put my words into practice, you're more aware of just how much you are loved by God, how to look critically at your expectations and how to lean on the coaching and advice from people in your world. Now for *the other person*. Where do you find this person, and what do you do once you find him or her?

The better prepared you are, the more fun dating can be. Dating itself begins with the three aforementioned topics: connecting to God; yourself; your community. If you've skipped forward to this section without reading the others, then you're missing a bit of the context. Just as a mountain climber doesn't begin with climbing the Himalayas, a first-time dater mustn't immediately want to marry. You learn step by step, and step by step you'll find yourself at the top of the mountain.

There are several things to consider when it comes to dating. First of all, you were made with more or less pre-existing attributes such as your appearance, personality, beliefs and values. There are also qualities you can grow or alter. For example, you have control over your mindset as you begin to date: will you flirt or take the imitative; what boundaries do you consider important; how will you deal with rejection? Finally there are things *outside* yourself to consider: how intentional are you with meeting new singles or avoiding them; how many other single people do you choose to have contact with and what types; how do you interact with them?

THE PERFECT FIT

Often you hear people say 'I just want to be accepted for who I am' or 'I'm looking for someone who suits me.' This approach assumes that we are who we are and that our personality is relatively stable. You often hear this idea spoken in terms of small children: 'This is really just his temperament' or 'She's been this easy-going since she was born.' These kinds of personal characteristics are important to consider if you're looking for a good match.

The latest research seems to show that couples who are matched through the internet tend to have a higher chance of success than couples who have simply found each other. Some of this is probably nonsense and perhaps based on research funded by the dating sites themselves, but there is something to this finding. There are sites that match couples based on personality traits, which may explain this reported success. Because however true the aphorism 'opposites attract' might be, it is the similarities that make a relationship last. And that's exactly why these internet sites match you: to avoid the outcome of sitting across the table from someone with whom you have little in common, and a relationship with little chance of success.

PERSONALITY

Approximately one half of your personality is formed by the time you are born, the other half developing throughout the course of your life.[1] Some character qualities are more sensitive to change than others. The most insightful and widely used personality test is the 'Big Five', the five biggest dimensions of personality on which people can be tested. One of the ways it is being used is in the pre-marriage material for the research-supported programme PREPARE/ENRICH – <www.prepare-enrich.com> (see Table 1).

What does Table 1 show? On the whole, the stronger the match within these categories, the greater the chance for a successful relationship. An exception is the category 'Emotional stability'. A low score on this scale undermines all types of relationships. People who quickly panic or have anxiety issues usually ask too much of their partner, or they turn her or him – usually him – down.

A high degree of neurotic behaviour can make a relationship difficult, also because communication is thereby more difficult. Under stress, we tend to make less contact with people or lose our ability to articulate what we want or think. In order really to connect with another person you have to be relaxed. Too many people get caught up in their own fears. Often people who have experienced singleness for a long time find themselves sinking into a mire of crippling fear. This fear keeps you from thinking rationally and therefore increases the probability of making unwise decisions.

Myra (36) was such a person. She came to my office because of depression but it turned out that Myra had been in relationship after relationship, rejecting each of the men she dated. Her current boyfriend also didn't appear good enough: 'He's not thoughtful,'

Table 1 Big Five personality traits

	High	Low
Social	High scorers are people who love social environments; they feel at home around others and become energized from attending social gatherings. These people are extraverts and their mood is quickly affected by circumstances.	Low scorers are people who are more reserved and introverted. Socially introverted people are often calmer, think more over their decisions and have a smaller social network. They prefer to be alone or with a few good friends. These people receive energy from being alone.
Flexibility	High scorers love change, are flexible, innovative and open to new experiences. They often have varied interests. They receive energy by thinking of creative and new solutions.	Low scorers love structure and predictability. They love things to stay the way they are and are level-headed and clear.
Organizational	High scorers are methodical and well organized. They are often tenacious and reliable, and place a high value on those qualities. They are quite deliberate and have a careful plan to achieve their goals.	Low scorers are chaotic and place a low value on schedules and structure. Their houses and workspaces are often untidy. They place more value on spontaneous activities than on well-planned ones.
Personal	High scorers are friendly, approachable and warm. They work well with others. They don't always have definite boundaries. They are loyal friends and partners.	Low scorers love a bit of distance. To be seen as friendly and personal is less important than being clear in what they want and don't want.
Emotionally stable	High scorers are calm and able to handle stress well. They experience few negative feelings, such as fear, sadness or anger.	Those who score low are sensitive and have strong reactions to stress. They don't always appreciate new situations and tend to avoid excitement. They experience a lot of fear, anger and sadness when things go wrong.

she complained, 'he never buys me flowers.' That didn't sound so bad to me (considering how inattentive Dutch guys can be), but hey – it was bothering her. 'What is the problem?' I asked. 'Well, a girlfriend of mine says that I can do better,' she confessed. 'And the friend,' I pressed, 'is she . . . ?' 'She's single!' Myra laughed: 'Okay, okay, I get it. But I'm so scared that I will sell myself short.'[2]

The reverse can also be true. When Chantal (31) asked for my help due to her social anxiety, it appeared that she wasn't afraid of engaging with men: 'They come to me, and I'm afraid to say "no".' Chantal had been seriously neglected as a child by a mentally ill father and an unstable mother. She had never learned what it means for someone to devote time and attention to you, what it means to be seen, heard and understood. What little attention she got meant so much to her; she deemed it normal to be neglected. As a result she had very low self-esteem; she was also very fearful, but instead of keeping everyone at a distance she let everyone in – to the point she became deeply in debt by loaning money to her previous boyfriend, who had an irrepressible desire to spend. She didn't dare say 'no' to his endless requests for money, for fear of being rejected, alone and neglected again.

A low score on emotional stability is something you can change. You can develop in this area by learning how to live: choosing healthy boundaries; developing your boundaries; learning about all dimensions of your emotions, fear included. Here a mental health professional can be especially helpful.

PHYSICAL APPEARANCE

It should be clear that dating is not about the physical, as we've learned in the previous chapter. Dating is about character, about someone's inner qualities. However, the physical appearance *is* the first thing you see. Physical appearance is important! People who look like slobs shouldn't complain when they find themselves either not dating or only dating other people who look like slobs.

Look in the mirror. Maybe invite someone from your team to do this with you. Do you like what you see? Does your hair look nice? Do your socks match? Do you wear clothes that fit your figure and colours that look attractive on you? These are actually important questions. You can only make a first impression once. Research shows that people who date place enormous amount of worth on the first impression.

Of course, this doesn't mean that you need to have the smallest build as a woman in order to be beautiful, or as a man have the broadest shoulders. People come in all shapes and sizes – a good thing, that allows a little diversity in choosing a partner. Perhaps initially it would be interesting if we all looked like Brad Pitt or Angelina Jolie, but in the end it would also be a bit confusing and tremendously boring.

If you have a little bit of a belly or are already balding, or you're rather short or have bad skin, or all of the above, there is no good reason to become a hermit. If you'd like, change what you can by working out, losing weight, cutting your hair or finding a good dermatologist. But above all else, accept and learn to love what simply is. Be proud of what you have to offer, and don't attach too much importance to what others might think.

As part of my dating course, I always invite a personal stylist to the last session, along with a spiritual director. The physical appearance is directly affected by the inner person. Our personal stylist takes a good look at the natural beauty someone already has, and tries to emphasize what's there. This often has surprising results. Karen told me with sparkling eyes:

> I thought this guy I saw at the dating course looked unattractive with his faded baggy jeans and over-gelled hair. But now that he's seen the stylist, all of a sudden he has these great clothes and hip hairstyle. I thought he was a really nice guy but now I find him really ... attractive!

Nothing wrong with enhancing what nature has given. When you're looking around, are you really trying to look your best?

Most importantly: you are sending a subliminal message through your appearance. Someone who doesn't care for his or her body, has unbrushed teeth or unkempt hair perhaps won't care that well for you. If brushing one's teeth or going to the barber or buying new clothes is already too difficult a task, how will it be when you're in a relationship with that person and you need him or her to care for you?

WHAT YOU CAN CHANGE

Consider what you can change about yourself to make your experience of singleness and dating more enjoyable. You should accept yourself as you are to a certain extent, but it's important to realize that there is also work to do. What is it you'd really like to change for the better about yourself?

MINDSET: IT'S NOT ABOUT GETTING MARRIED!

The first and biggest change that helped me in my concept of relationships was the thought that dating isn't about getting married; dating is about daring to encounter someone else. The concern over whether we'll marry or not comes later. Earlier in my dating life I had continuously analysed things throughout the date, trying to determine whether or not it would develop into a long-term relationship. Eventually I decided to let that go. I no longer had to decide immediately if this was 'it' for the long term, or if this date would just be a one-time event. In the end, the only thing I had to conclude by the end of the date was whether or not there would be another one. Such a relief!

Every marriage begins with one date but the fact remains that the majority of dates won't result in marriage. This is a good thing. Dating with marriage in mind may result in dates that feel forced, tense situations in which people find it difficult to be their best, true selves. Dating with the end – marriage – in mind doesn't do justice to yourself or to the other person.

In the first place, dates with this kind of pressure just aren't fair to the other person, because often it allows that person only one chance to prove him or herself. 'That's what it often feels like!' admitted Bert (34). 'I have *one* chance to make an impression on a woman. One chance to do it right, or screw up. One chance to prove myself, to put my cards on the table. And that really makes me nervous.' For Bert it was a huge relief to give himself permission to date just to date, without immediately having to measure up to some impossibly high standard.

If you demand a high standard of yourself, whether or not you're aware of it, you're also demanding a high standard of the other person. You want to get to know someone as he or she is but how can that person comfortably be his or herself if you're not comfortably yourself? And what do you then really see in the other person? You won't have a complete picture but you will see enough if your date is free and relaxed enough to be his or herself.

Finally, dating with marriage in mind doesn't do justice to marriage itself. When you marry, you marry a real person made of flesh and blood, beautiful and broken. You degrade marriage if you treat it as something that's of your own making or something you can completely control, especially if you think you can draw a conclusion about someone by the end of one date. Marriage is a beautiful but complex partnership. It's not just about checking 'marry' off your to-do list. 'Allow all four seasons to pass before you decide to marry' is often the advice given. And good advice doesn't appear out of thin air. Only as time passes do you see more and more of who someone is within your developing relationship.

The heart of the matter is this: marriage is a dynamic process between two people. It's not only the momentary 'I do' that you say on your wedding day, and then it's settled. It is indeed something that is alive and growing. Think of a tree: a tree is a tree from the time it is a small sapling peeking above the surface of the earth, and a tree is a tree when it's standing tall with its thick trunk and rustling leaves. A marriage is just like a tree; it lives, it grows and it continually changes and develops. It also needs careful care and nourishment in order to do that, especially in the beginning.

FLIRTING

Let's say you find yourself at a conference about the topic of God and work. It's fascinating, of course, but you have a second secret agenda: to meet other single people. Then, wait a minute, you see an attractive woman. Should you go for it? What if she's in a relationship? You peek at her hands. Nope, no ring. Now for an opening line. You hesitate, beginning to sweat a little, but before you can make a move, someone else gets there first. Too late. On to the next available woman then.

You will have to be more open if you want to take Chapter 2's assignment seriously and 'Meet five new single people per week'. This means paying more attention to your surroundings. Maybe you will notice that shy man on the train you often overlook, or finally say hello to that quiet woman at church, even though you would have ignored her before now. And sure enough, she says 'Hello' back.

For a man this often implies making contact: initiating contact with women who appear interesting; sending an email to the woman who has a nice online profile; or beginning a conversation with that woman in the church. Often men are afraid to be seen as 'a player', and for women an equal fear is being classified as 'a flirt'. But there is a whole range of possibilities between sitting alone at home and running around batting your eyelids at everyone. Simply being kind and friendly isn't the same as shameless flirting. And even if you do find yourself flirting a bit, that's all right!

Women can sometimes be so terrified to give men the wrong idea that their attitude can become too defensive. 'I've learned to smile at guys', Christine told me. 'And really, just smiling has gotten me about one date per week.' Christine had never dated because of her fear that men didn't find her attractive. Now that she had learned to smile, Christine did this more and more naturally. So when her future husband sat on the chair next to her at church, in his own words: 'I would never have talked to her if she hadn't looked at me in such a friendly way. And I'm not the bravest guy. But with her, things just flowed naturally.'

Everyone is more attractive when they smile. The simple act of smiling makes you approachable, softer. 'I consider it a kind of miracle', Laura from Chapter 2 told me later. She was given the same advice. 'It really makes quite a big difference. I see it with myself as well; smiling makes me more accessible.' The men dating Laura confirmed this. 'She's a lot of fun, good company, and puts you at ease. That made it easy to approach her,' the man who is now her husband told me: 'I saw her standing there and immediately thought, "Wow, she's great!" I was immediately a fan.'

Ladies: discover your inner flirt. Are you shy? Practise smiling and really look someone in the eye. Count to three in your head if that helps. Even better: first look at someone for one second, look away, and then look back for three seconds. Now it may sound like a short amount of time but it feels really long. And I've seen it do wonders.

Is flirting okay with God? I was asked that question once at a workshop. Why not? The idea that people should feel ashamed by just being friendly and open to each other makes me sad. Have we forgotten how to be friendly to each other because we are so afraid of the consequences? A little bit of flirting is not the same as shameless, pushy flirtation. I disapprove of excessive flirtation unless the person you're interested in is completely blind. Some men simply need a bit more encouragement than others.

I ask the men similar questions: 'Are you a player?' Then you probably wouldn't have picked up this book. But if you are, what makes you a player, and how can you change this? Are you shy? What helps you come out of your shell? You don't need to throw yourself at the feet of women but what can you do to make more contact with them? Do you dare to take action?

INITIATIVE

What women often say they find attractive in a man can be summed up in one word: initiative. 'If he approaches me with a good idea for a date'; 'When he says he cares for me.' It sounds so simple but it can be really very exciting. Women love a man with a plan. Try it! And remember this motto: if you're rejected often, then at least you're doing something right – you're taking plenty of initiative!

Sometimes when men think of taking the initiative they think they need to assume a James Bond type of bravado. This is sometimes the image that books written for men promote: a rugged masculinity, involving some sort of survival trip. In the UK and elsewhere there is Christian Vision for men, and in the USA, Church for Men is active. When I see how these organizations and their initiatives work for many men, it's about finding a balance between daring to be strong and confident, and allowing that strength and confidence to make contact with others. This returns to the true essence of strength, as God's creation intended.

Earlier in my work, I paid more attention to the role of men in the Church and I discovered that it's often not a popular place for men, especially single men. Often the Church can be too sentimental. I also found that women too often want to date the kind of man described as metrosexual. They cringe if a man doesn't both show great intelligence *and* ask highly empathetic questions about their stress level, mother or annoying boss. Some men are more sensitive than others but that's all right, especially if you also can see they've got strength and initiative. 'Let them just be themselves' is what I've told more than one single girlfriend.

Some of them are more sensitive than others but that's just fine. It's time to stop complaining about those out-of-style shoes or silly jokes.

SETTING BOUNDARIES

I have already mentioned this in previous chapters, but dating is really a question of setting healthy boundaries. Dating involves the risk of heartbreak and making mistakes. Dating involves risking hurt but doesn't need to be damaging if you date within healthy boundaries.

What are these healthy boundaries? Here's a list:

1   Be yourself – there's no other way to be in a relationship. This is a good place to begin.
2   Be honest – do you have the sense that someone too often makes decisions on your behalf? Sits too close to you? Is too quick to share very personal information? Tell them! Be honest and clear, but kind. Tell them what you like and what you don't like.
3   Share your dating philosophy – tell him or her if you'd prefer to date more than one person at a time, for example. Or if you'd like to keep things light, dating can mean doing fun activities together and seeing where things go from there; dating doesn't have to lead to a marriage proposal.
4   Meet in a public place – this way you can be sure that the level of intimacy remains appropriate for the occasion, and it ensures that you're safe.
5   Don't give too much information too quickly. This is also helpful in protecting yourself. Keep private things private unless and until you're sure you'd like to continue the relationship.

It's strange how quickly we can lose sight of our boundaries if we're attracted to someone. You throw caution to the wind and tend to go all-in. This is often the result of infatuation hormones but usually this is not a healthy reaction. You'll be ashamed and sorry about what you've shared – too much, too soon – if things don't move in the direction of a relationship.

Dare to reject, kindly. Dare to tell someone that you don't want to continue to date them, and if they ask, also why you've arrived at that decision. Try to formulate an answer that begins with yourself. 'I told him that I didn't want to keep dating him because I didn't feel safe with him,' commented Annelise (31):

> He kept making comments about women and touched me a bit too much, which I found creepy. This feedback really shocked him. I don't think that was his intention but I thought he had better know why I didn't want to go on a second date with him.

'Oh yes, I know that type,' sighed Annelise's girlfriend, who sat with us in the conversation:

> I once had a date with a man who kept making jokes about foreigners. He was probably saving his commentary about women for the second date. Too bad that I didn't tell him why I didn't want a second date.

Annelise did that man quite a favour by being honest with him. Some people are simply not aware of their behaviour, and this is where honest feedback about how behaviour affects others can be extraordinarily helpful. But in order for this to have a positive effect, be careful how you give the feedback – it should be in the form of constructive criticism rather than damaging critique.

DEALING WITH REJECTION

Rejection is a part of the deal. You cannot keep dating everyone for ever. But the reality is that people often have difficulty with rejection. Of course it's never fun, and it will never be easy. But it's helpful to look at the bigger perspective.

Compare it to buying shoes. (Granted, this example may be a feminine one but it's helpful nonetheless. Stay with me, gentlemen. Maybe replace the word 'shoes' with 'car'.) When you go to the store, sometimes you can find five pairs of shoes that serve your purpose and fit you. Yet there are only one or two that will make you really happy. Why is that? Well, it can be because of that one detail – that exact colour or how the shoe feels on your foot. Even if you and your girlfriend have the same taste and wear the same size, the chance is still high that she'll choose another pair. Why? The same story. It could be anything – a detail, and the colour. There is something small but significant that causes each of you to decide on different shoes. And that is splendid, because if it didn't turn out this way you might find yourselves arguing over who buys that one pair. Does that mean that the other shoes are flawed? No, of course not! And when it comes to relationships, does rejection mean that you are not all right? No, it just means that you may find a better fit with someone else you prefer.

If you can see it this way, rejection will be easier to accept. And it will also become easier to reject someone else. You're not rejecting the person as a whole, you're rejecting the possibility of their being suitable for an intimate relationship. Maybe you'll become friends but perhaps you never want to see this person again. However, the chance is pretty small that you really dislike the whole person.

The reverse is also true. Someone can think you're attractive and fun and smart but still choose not to begin a relationship with you. Never give someone the power to decide whether you're an okay person or not! Rejection is a part of life. Learn to deal with it. Jason (38) told me:

> Because I learned how to accept rejection as a part of the process of dating, I can also deal better with rejection when I'm applying for jobs. I now understand that rejection comes with the territory, and nine times out of ten it's nothing personal.

'But if a relationship may end up as nothing, and I anticipate that might be the case, why should I even try?', challenged a woman called Maggie (45) one day. 'Because you don't know how it will turn out,' I answered. There are more than enough people who married outside their 'type'. They hardly even remember what their original type was unless you ask for it: 'Oh, that's right. I wasn't that into the small and blonde type. But that all changed when I met her.'

Actually you should be grateful for your bad dating experiences. Knowledge about what you don't want is also knowledge. If you date all kinds of people then you'll have to reject a lot. You'll also have a lot to be thankful for, because after dating all kinds of people you're better able to know who bests suits you. The person who can't take a little rejection shouldn't be dating.

DEALING WITH INFATUATION

'If I fall for someone after a first date, then what?' That is the most widely searched topic on the Dare to Date website. I find this fascinating. Why? Is it really such a problem to find yourself falling for someone after one date?

If you find yourself immediately infatuated, ask yourself two questions: 'Who am I falling for?' 'Why am I falling for this person?' Are you really seeing the other person as he or she is or are you seeing what you want to see? Those might not be fun questions but they're definitely relevant ones. Think back to Diana from Chapter 1. She fell quickly in love and found the experience wonderful – until a few weeks had passed and the rose-tinted glasses began to come off and she could see what was really happening: she was dating someone who, in no time, had crossed her boundaries. And just like that, the love was gone. Because Diana had so quickly poured herself into the relationship, the break-up cost her more sadness and tears than if she had begun more cautiously.

Hollywood plays a trick on us when it comes to the idea of love and infatuation. If it's in a film, why can't it also be in real life? Two people see each other and are immediately in love. And after a few more or less predictable obstacles, they end up together and live happily ever after. Think about it. Each romantic comedy follows more or less the same story. Margaret told me:

> I had just started dating him, and right away I had big reservations about our relationship. I wasn't super 'in love'. I talked with my pastor about it, and he told me to stop watching romantic comedies, reading romance novels or daydreaming about the ideal love for one year. 'It messes with your mind,' he said, 'and gives you a distorted perspective of relationships.' His advice definitely helped me. I had never really noticed how unrealistically the films' relationships

were depicted and how attractive people always looked. I learned to value real life, what Ari and I actually had. So now we've been married 12 years, and I'm so grateful for the advice given then.

Unlike real life, the infatuation portrayed in the cinema often involves someone who is completely different from you. Differences are thrilling, and this excitement gives your body a sort of heightened sense of awareness, making it easier for you to mistake your feelings for infatuation. 'I thought my husband was really boring when I first met him,' Heidi said. 'I mean, I didn't think he was unattractive but I didn't think "Wow" right away.' That 'wow' feeling is what a lot of singles are looking for on that first date. But the wow feeling is misleading. If you're falling for someone after a first date, it's probable that you're in love with your own idea of who the other person might be. In love after the first date? Watch out!

First, sit with your team around the table. Let them ask you questions. Go out with the person a few more times. Infatuation comes and goes. What's even more important is to see the real person who is sitting across from you. For some people the wow feeling is a good enough reason to begin a relationship, and it gives the energy needed during the process of getting to know a person. But sometimes it is not a good sign.

PLACES TO MEET

The first question people often ask when I talk about the various dates I've been on is 'Where do you get your ideas?' Five years ago I wouldn't have known. Now I see possibilities everywhere (and my single years of dating are over!).

If you take a look at unmarried people in the Bible, then you often find that most of them met their future husband or wife at the well. The village watering hole was often a place of meeting. Everyone from the community came to talk over the news, exchange gossip or enjoy the day. And so the well was a place to meet others.

The truth is, you shouldn't only be *looking* for dates, you should also be making it easier for others to *find you*. Go where other single people are. 'Increasing my findability', I always called it, which is also one of the reasons I subscribed to a dating website. I'll also list a few places here, but with a warning. Simply finding people is not the answer. Too often churches – or dating sites! – speak in terms of finding a 'solution' for their single members: 'We need to organize a social event so that they can meet each other.' There are more than enough places to meet, if you're looking. However, what's far more important is how you act, think and feel during these encounters with other people. With that in mind, below are a few tips on where you can meet others.

CHURCH

Church is the most logical place for Christians to find a partner. Of course, this depends on what kind of church you're part of. Are there just families or do single people also come regularly? If you want to enlarge your network, it can beneficial to go every now and then to a church that many singles attend.

Many single people I know do just that. They're regular attenders of their home church but also visit churches that include larger numbers of single people. There they meet new people or get to know others better. It's not a bad idea.

'Doesn't that make you a bit of an obsessive single?' people sometimes ask. Ellen (42) met her husband by organizing regular events for singles:

> Definitely not obsessive, but fun! I had lots of fun at those parties. Once I invited 15 unmarried girlfriends and told them each to bring an unmarried man. From that event we've had several couples come about. I wanted to get married, so I decided to do something about it.

Andrea (28) told me about the dinner parties she regularly organizes:

> We brought six men and six women together and everyone took responsibility for a different part of the meal. It was so much fun, and there were all kinds of combinations of dates that came out of the dinner parties. What's great is that it's not about if relationships form because of this idea, but that we're expanding our networks and you see that really happening. We're also much more aware of some cool singles in our community, people we had overlooked before. Now I'll look around and think 'I'd like to have dinner with that person.'

I know that in many big-city church communities there are more singles than people might think. A tip is to keep the singles events to as much of a 50:50 men-to-women ratio as you can. That ensures that the atmosphere within the group stays relaxed and balanced, which helps avoid those circumstances in which all the women jump on the three men in the group, and ensures that everyone talks with everyone. And if the group is a bit larger, you can prevent everyone from paying too much attention to what others are up to and encourage the group just to have fun.

Another advantage of church is that the people who meet there live in your neighbourhood. I know three separate couples who met each other via an internet dating website but discovered that they'd lived in the same city for years. That may only be possible in the Netherlands because we live in such a tiny country; but still, proximity is an important factor in the development of relationships. You will be quicker to meet someone for coffee who lives in the same region than someone who lives on the other side of the country.

CONFERENCES, EVENTS AND SO ON

Is your church a bit short of singles? Search for events for people in your age group. Or look for conferences whose themes spark your interest. There's a good chance that you'll meet people there with whom you have things in common.

'I really didn't want to go with my friends to that conference,' admitted Harry (46):

> I was 33, single, and I definitely wanted a girlfriend, but it hadn't happened and so I'd given up a little. And then some friends told me: 'Come on, Harry: just go. There are really lovely women going.' So I went rather unwillingly. But what do you know, the speaker was really good, and secretly I thought to myself: 'You never know.' The next morning I woke up and went to breakfast. A woman was sitting there who was also early, so I sat next to her. We talked the whole day, and now we've been married for 12 years. I still think it's so incredible how I met her!

From my perspective, Harry's story doesn't seem *that* incredible. These kinds of places often have some great single people; it just takes sitting down next to someone at the breakfast table. Here's another tip: go alone. Don't go with your friends, or if you go with friends, don't stay in the same group the entire time. Get out there by yourself! Be daring and sit by yourself. Who knows if someone might sit next to you? Try finding someone sitting alone and sit next to him or her. Who knows? You might find yourself in a good conversation.

Good places to meet might also include the supermarket, the train station or the pub. It's true that public places aren't always the best ones in which to meet other Christians, but it doesn't hurt to be alert to the people and conversations around you. This helps you with that first exercise of making contact with new people, and gives you a good chance to practise. Opportunities to meet people are all around you; it's your responsibility just to show up.

THE INTERNET

Dating websites can be a goldmine to help you practise. You don't have to join expecting to meet the person you will marry, but see it as a sort of relaxed place where you have the opportunity to meet other Christian singles. The sites definitely increase your chances of meeting people. And everyone who is there is Christian and single. What more can you ask for, and what have you got to lose?

It isn't enough simply to have a profile on a dating website. I spoke with two male friends, both single, one who is 36 and has never been married, and the other who is 42 and divorced: 'And are you both still on a dating site?' I asked. 'Oh, sure,' they both admitted. 'And how many women do you message per week?'

'How many? What do you mean? I look around.' 'You look *around*?' 'Yeah, I look around. And sometimes I get a message.' The men began to shift uncomfortably in their chairs. 'What do you mean by *I look around*? How long have you had a profile on the site?' I looked from one to the other. 'Um, three years, I think.' 'Okay,' I pushed on, 'and in those three years, how many women have you messaged?' There was a long pause. 'Maybe ... three?' one friend offered cautiously. 'Not enough?' My mouth fell open: 'Three – really? Are you serious? In three years? So one per year?' Bachelor Number One blinked at me and said: 'Yeah. Why?'

These men really couldn't explain to me why they had so little activity on their dating sites. Fear? Shyness? The possibility of being rejected? Regardless of the reason, this encounter was in sharp contrast to my conversation with another male friend. Louis (33) told me:

> I just message anyone who looks like fun. Sometimes I get a message back, and often I don't. But it's not the number of responses that interests me. I've been on quite a few dates and now I'm in a relationship with a woman I met on the site. And we're really happy.

I think Louis's strategy is a good one. Just send a message and go for it. Don't allow fear to hold you back. Rejection via the internet is not rejection. If someone doesn't message you back, then it's very possible they're simply a rude jerk or a high-maintenance diva. There simply wasn't an attraction and you can move on to the next message. There's nothing less personal than being rejected on a dating site.

Think about it. From a website profile, someone can only know a tiny percentage of all of the information there is to know about you. It's far more important whether you find the person attractive in real life. He or she should be someone with whom you feel comfortable, someone with whom you can share good conversations – or even someone who behaves well in a restaurant. Speaking of her husband, a friend admitted that:

> I didn't find him that fascinating until our second date, when he discerned that I was sitting close to the parade of people coming in and out of the restaurant. He offered to switch chairs with me so I would be more comfortable. All of a sudden I thought: 'Hey, you pay attention. You know how to take care of me.' It seems like something so small but it was an important moment for me.

Of course, details such as age and education are relevant to some extent but in the end they give such little information about the *person*. To determine whether or not you feel at home with someone is a whole other experience. Dare to read between the lines and look beyond the details. Dare to return someone's message; dare to take the initiative.

This also applies to women. If there's one place you can take the initiative, it's in internet dating. Here you're able simply to take a look at someone who looks like a potential match and send a message to them. Stalking his profile in the hope that some interesting-looking man initiates on his own can make you feel powerless, and you really don't need to sit and wait!

The following applies to both men and women: don't email back and forth with someone from a dating site for too long. Give yourself a three-time rule, and then meet in person. Don't give too many details through email, or share too much of yourself before you know who the other person is. Otherwise it's too easy to daydream about who you think someone might be, or more likely who you hope that someone will be. If your dreams aren't based on a real meeting, then you'll find yourself standing on thin ice.

Barbara (29) told me:

> We emailed for three months after meeting on a dating site. We had also spoken on the phone a few times. So of course I had formed an image of this guy. I thought that he would be really gallant and kind, helpful and attentive. I thought to myself 'This could be *the* guy.' When I finally met him in reality, he spent the whole time talking about himself. My subsequent disappointment was my own fault; I'd let my expectations get too high.

One final tip: If you meet someone you really like, don't immediately jump into topics such as past relationships, how many children you want or what you'd name the dog. Wait until you get to know each other better. It's not that these things aren't important but even a great person might be put off by such directness right at the start, and feel pressured. You might prevent a wonderful relationship from ever starting.

SPEED DATING

Speed dating has become a normal dating activity. At many large Christian conferences you can sign up for a speed-dating session but there are also sessions organized regularly by dating sites. Rabbi Yaacov Deyo, from New York, allegedly created speed dating when he noticed that quite a few Jewish parishioners were remaining single for longer periods of time.[3] To the rabbi, it seemed like an efficient way for people to meet.

It *can* be an efficient way to meet people. As Reina (27) said:

> A girlfriend of mine invited me to go speed dating with her. It seemed like fun to me, although I wasn't really looking. It seemed like a quick, efficient way to get to know men. Then I sat down across the table from Simon. We hit it off right away! I didn't think he was super attractive at first but I could really laugh with him. We found ourselves meeting again, and then a couple of more times, until I discovered that I really liked him. And now we've been married for two years.

Meeting a partner can work the way it did in Reina and Simon's case but overall the concept appears to be a bit complex for the human mind, as Barry Schwartz, an American psychologist, discovered when he set out to find out what too much choice can do to the human mind. In a supermarket, he set out jams for people to try. On days when there were only six choices, the jams sold far better than on the days when there were 24.[4] More choices don't automatically result in better choices.

Somebody once said at one of my seminars 'So what you're actually saying is that you should choose every person with whom you speed date for a follow up date?' Consequently, based on the principle of Henry Cloud to 'Go out with almost anyone once, and maybe again',[5] then yes: seeing a good number of them again may well be a good approach.

DATING DOS AND DON'TS

Here's a bit of practical advice. What are some useful dating tips? I've compiled the following list for you to consider:

DOS

- Be careful and be safe: always meet someone in a public place and make sure you let others know where you are and with whom.
- Before you leave for a date, make sure you verify your reasons for going. Take a deep breath and remind yourself that 'A date doesn't mean marriage. A date is about meeting another person, a brother, a sister, another child of God.'
- Don't just stay put – get out there! Don't go out to eat each time, especially not on the first date, because then you're sitting across from each other, which only serves to increase the tension. Go for a walk, to the zoo, visit a museum. Going out and doing something together is far more interesting and informative.
- Stay calm. Relax! Be yourself – that's when you're at your best.
- Take care to look good and maintain your appearance.
- Always take good care of yourself. You can't expect the other person to know how to do that for you. Be intentional in getting enough sleep and healthy food, and allow yourself time to recharge between dates.
- Be chivalrous (gentlemen) and allow yourselves to be treated this way (ladies). Hold the door open and allow the door to be opened for you. Take up the offer to wear his coat if you're cold.
- Offer to pay (ladies)! Pay (gentlemen)! Be clear about money (paying). Do you have a small budget? Discuss this in advance and either find something inexpensive to do or be clear about splitting the bill 50:50. This isn't about money, gentlemen

(women aren't usually trying to be gold diggers), this is about how cared-for women feel. And ladies, don't fight with him if he offers to pay. Simply smile and say 'Thank you.'

- Be on time. Again, the issue here isn't so much about whether you can tell the time but what message you're giving. If you're late, you're saying 'Our date isn't important enough for me to be on time; at least I'm here, right?' When you're on time, you're communicating 'You are important and this date is important.' You've already scored points.

- Take time to reflect on your dates. Take a look at the evaluation in the back of this book. After a good night's sleep, take some quiet time and reflect back on your date. What did you like? What did you not like? Ask this about yourself as well as the other person. What can you take with you for future dates when it comes to what you're looking or not looking for? Overall, try to focus on what you've experienced and felt, without focusing so much on drawing a conclusion. This is also less relevant in the long term. A date is not about adding up pros or cons. A date is a meeting between two people.

- Ring someone from your team and discuss the date.

- Communicate with the other person if there will be a second date or not, and the reasons why. It's disrespectful simply to drop all communication – no matter what. You don't necessarily need to call someone after a date but you can always send an email or text message.

- Have you had more than three dates? It's always all right to end it but that's when you should either call the person or meet up and explain why you don't want to continue dating. Ending a series of dates by text message is never all right!

- Do you want to continue dating someone? Read the next chapter ...

DON'TS

- Date according to a set of rules. In the USA the book *The Rules*, by Ellen Fein and Sherrie Schneider, was a *New York Times* bestseller.[6] The point, however, is not to make dating a game but to be real and sincerely yourself.
- Date more than one person at the same time. Hmm: I'm not so sure about this one. According to Henry Cloud, dating more than one person is fine and prevents you from focusing too much on just one. I've never succeeded doing this well myself, at least not to a point where I was satisfied. But frankly, I'm more traditional. It may be that you begin the day drinking coffee with Bachelor Number One and end up meeting Bachelor Number Two for dinner. In this case, be honest that you're seeing other people, which helps avoid disappointment.
- Stop after one date. Go on a second date with everyone and a third date with almost everyone. Of course, sometimes you may meet someone about whom you think 'Never again'. But most people are truly not their best on a first date. Just say 'yes' to a second date.
- Fantasize about how amazing somebody is. That doesn't help anybody.
- Talk about your parents to your date and mention their obsession to see you married. Weird and scary!
- Go to the cinema. Seriously. If you really want to get to know someone, then you don't want to spend two hours together

staring at a screen, unless you're both incredibly introverted. But still go out again and talk.

- Take yourself too seriously. Nothing is as unattractive as a man or woman who talks non-stop on the date about his or her work performance.
- Only begin to think about your boundaries and desires once you're in love. Set your boundaries in advance. More about that in the next chapter.
- Immediately send a text after a date. Of course, sending a short message that you've had a good time is fine. But I'm talking about stories of people sending anywhere from three to fourteen texts, phone calls and even dropping by. Don't be a stalker. Stalkers are scary. Give someone enough space to decide what he or she wants, if they want to continue.

The core message is this: be intentional about your actions and honest about your motivations. Make and implement a plan from start to finish. Know what you're doing. Dating is not something to do half-heartedly. Date with your mind and heart and allow your team to ask hard questions. This is the way to get the most from your experiences.

QUESTIONS FOR FURTHER REFLECTION

- What qualities do you find important in another person? Think about appearance, education, status and so on.
- Are you afraid of the expectations the other person may have of you? How do you deal with that?
- If you want to date someone from the church, do you find it annoying if other people from the church know about it?

Why or why not? Do the expectations of others around you play a role?

- How do you see your role as a man or a woman in the dating process? And what do you expect of a man if you're a woman, and vice versa? Are your expectations realistic?
- Can you date someone you're already friends with? Why or why not?
- How can you be more open and inviting?
- Should a woman ask a man out?

ASSIGNMENTS

- Date ten different types of people – the philosopher, the artist, the businessman, the girl next door, the fashion model, the nerd and so on – and then see if your 'type' has changed.
- Reflect on your dates using the evaluation sheet in the Appendix.

5 Finding your match: now what?

And all of a sudden – it's happened. What's next? Exclusive dating? How do you talk about that together? What are some of the other relational phases you can expect? And when do you start thinking about marriage?

TAKE YOUR TIME

If you decide to begin to date someone exclusively, many of the same principles still apply. You still need to pursue connection with God, yourself, the people around you and with each other. More strongly put: a good relationship should serve to deepen your other relationships. It brings you closer to yourself, to God, to friends and family.

'A relationship is an adventure,' a good friend of mine told me when I began dating the man who is now my husband: 'You've got to take it step by step and reject the impulse to sprint to the finish line.' Her words were an enormous help. Taking it step by step is often not the first priority of Western culture. Our generation seems to say 'I want it all and I want it now.' But let's not blame it too much on 'the spirit of the times'.

Patience is not really my forte but luckily I was able to put it into practice during my single years. During the process of a growing relationship you will go through several phases; it is important to take your time in each of these. It's also important in every phase to use your brain, asking yourself good questions. Of course, feelings remain an important factor but you must also use your brain to reflect over what is happening between the two of you, whether you feel safe and free and so on.

All of this takes time. Getting to know someone doesn't just happen on its own. Many single people have the idea that finding a relationship means that you've arrived, that it's a matter of finding the right person, and once you've done that the relationship will thrive. Many married people, however, know that it's far more a matter of growth. It helps to find a good partner but what happens between you two is really a question of growth. Compare it again to a tree. If an acorn falls to the ground, it doesn't immediately become an oak tree. A beautiful, stately oak requires decades to grow.

Take the time a relationship needs to grow in a healthy way, deciding what matters and practising the kind of life you want to live, even if you're older and feeling pressure to move quickly.

As I've said, I'm not the most patient person. I love gardening but as soon as I plant a seed, I return the next day to see if there's evidence of the new little plant growing. I do this despite the knowledge that first a seed must germinate and root before it can come above the soil. The image of a plant's growth really helped me in the early months of my relationship with my husband. I had recently brought hollyhock seeds back with me from a vacation in France. Hollyhocks are biennial plants, meaning their first blooms can't be seen until the second year after planting. So with the hollyhock seeds my patience was especially tested. To help myself remember that a relationship must and will take time, I planted these seeds. The slowly growing plant reassured me. He and I grew too.

On the other hand, too many people wait endlessly for their partner finally to make a decision regarding the relationship. Women, especially, seem too often to be *too* patient with their boyfriend's hesitancy to commit. Do yourself a favour and at a certain point, give him an ultimatum. Of the most beautiful passages I've read from Timothy Keller's *The Meaning of Marriage* is the 'pearls before swine' speech. After years of friendship, Keller's wife Kathy told him something along the lines of:

> Look. You've got to make a decision. You know the biblical story about the pearls being tossed in front of the swine? If you don't see my value by now, I'm not going to wait until you finally decide what you want out of this relationship.[1]

This is also about boundaries. If you're fine with a three-year engagement without clear future plans, all right. But if you want to know where your relationship is moving, then it's time for an honest conversation. Keller and his wife see this happen regularly. 'Don't let things get too passionate too quickly,' says Keller: 'However, also don't become a faux spouse for someone who won't commit to you.' He calls it the 'cheap girlfriend syndrome'.[2] This is another area where it's good to set limits.

Some men and women are simply unaware of how bad a certain relationship is for them. If you find yourself crying on the sofa after every date, there is something awry, no matter how much 'potential' someone may appear to have. You're not her father, or his mother. Furthermore, good fathers and mothers are meant to let their children leave the nest. If you've raised them well, they're ready to fly. This is also often true for people who want to 'rescue' their dates. If they're successful, ultimately they will probably end up being abandoned themselves.

When Elsa (30) told me about her sixth date with Sean, she said: 'I wasn't really that happy after the date but I saw so much potential in him!' Immediately alarms bells went off in my head: 'What do you mean by "potential"? I asked. 'Well, he's smart, sweet, attentive, kind, and funny!' 'But . . . ?' 'She answered: 'It's just that he's had a difficult childhood.' Whenever a man or woman says this kind of thing to me, my response is to look him or her straight in the face and say 'Think *very* carefully about this. Your Messiah Complex is playing a role. It's not up to you to rescue this person. He/she needs to go to therapy to work through his/ her difficult childhood.'

Dirk (48) said something similar about his relationship with Janice: 'She was so sweet and pretty, so fun in the beginning,' he said.

> But that quickly changed. She became needy, demanding more of my attention. She could also be unbelievably mean, saying really ugly things. So then I thought I should do what Jesus would. Accept her. She can't help it; she's just been raised this way. Until I reached a place where I couldn't do it any more. I literally fell apart. And that's when I put a stop to it.

Fortunately, Dirk had learned how to establish boundaries from previous relationships. He had the added benefit of a team that was there for him. But even though that relationship had only lasted three months, this experience affected Dirk deeply: 'Since then I've been dating someone else,' he told me, smiling. Becoming more serious, he added: 'But it's been difficult for me to trust her. However, trust is certainly growing.'

PHASES IN DATING

To help you remember which phases you may have within a relationship, I use an 'ABC' memory tool. The 'A' stands for 'attentive listening', the 'B' is for 'basic commitment', laying the foundation on which your relationship is based , and the 'C' is for 'choice', deciding whether or not you want to continue with the relationship. And there is a bonus 'D', as you will find out. This process of going through all the phases can take an average of one and a half to two years to complete. The more mature you both are, the faster the process can be, in principle. If you're both young and still studying, than take all the time you need. But if after three years you still haven't made a decision, then ask yourself what you're really doing.

Usually the phases come one after the other but every now and then you can switch phases. Sometimes all of your doubts seem to disappear and you move forward, only to find yourself reconsidering your decision two weeks later. It seems that often the same doubts return, but if the relationship is healthy, it can work like a spiral staircase. You may pass by the same point more than once but the intention is to go a bit deeper in your understanding with every step.

PHASE 1: 'A' FOR 'ATTENTIVE LISTENING' (AND BEING HEARD)

Attentive listening is a quality that as a therapist I had to work hard to develop. Listening is often a very hard thing to do well. It's difficult to understand someone completely from the beginning to the end. Try this. In your next conversation, take five minutes just to listen. And if you react, then use your words to reflect back to the person his or her own words and your understanding of what was said.

A good exercise from Nicky and Sila Lee's Marriage Preparation Course about how to be an attentive listener is the following:

> Take a random problem, not too big, and allow the other person to talk about all of their thoughts and feelings. Remember to ask questions about what they've said, just long enough to really understand the problem fully through the other person's eyes.[3]

As a therapist I often have to bite my tongue to avoid reacting too quickly to what someone says. But if you really want the other to feel listened to, at the beginning of a relationship you should be in a questioning phase: 'Who are you?' 'What is your personality?' 'What are your beliefs and what is your background?' These are important things to know about someone before you can decide if you want to continue the relationship.

You also want to know things like: 'Who are the people who have influenced you?' 'What is your stance in life?' 'What is important to you?' 'How do you see the future?' There are endless possible questions you can ask. In this phase, it is often best to spend as much time as possible simply listening and responding.

On dating sites, some profiles include similar questions. Karen, who has since then married, told me: 'The questions were already posed in a Christian dating website profile page. I used the answers people had put during dates, as a bit of a talking point.' It helped her to focus on asking good questions if she felt nervous on a date.

That being said, give your date his or her space. As Elsa said about her latest date: 'I want to know everything about him, everything! And as quickly as possible. So I have this book of questions, where we can choose what we want to discuss.' If this particular man is fine with this, then great. But it shouldn't be forced. Most men don't enjoy being interrogated or pressed to put all their cards on the table.

At this stage it's important to give yourself the space to have second thoughts. Doubting can be helpful. Healthy doubts are a sign that you're taking your encounters with someone seriously. Talk about what's bothering you, preferably with the person themselves. 'I don't like how he tends to withdraw at parties,' my friend Anne told me:

> He doesn't seem to be having a good time, and he isn't involved in much of the conversation. But when I talked with him about it, it seems like he's just a bit shy, especially in large groups. He would like to be different in this area. Our talk helped me to understand him better. And I really do see him coming out of his shell.

The difficult thing about doubt is that you often don't want to feel it. 'I almost panicked,' Miriam told me: 'I thought, "You see, I'm second-guessing. This isn't good. I've got to end it." But I didn't want to end it. Not because I wanted the relationship to continue but because I wasn't over the relationship.' Gradually Miriam realized that her doubts were resurfacing at certain times. If he came home from work and was really tired, failing to engage with her properly, then she felt left alone. 'And then I could be really critical. I would start making nasty comments or articulating my doubts.' When she could articulate to her boyfriend Rick how insecure his silence made her, he could then attempt to reach out to her instead of feeling rejected by her sharp criticism. As a result, her doubts slowly subsided. However, this process lasted a number of months.

Of course, someone must also listen attentively to you. This is the nature of communication. It's one of the most important qualities to have if you want to grow old happily with someone. And it's not only about who you marry but more about how you deal with your differences – how you talk about what you're struggling with and how open the person is to hearing it. If you find yourself with someone but you can't talk about real things, then it will be difficult – if your partner quickly feels threatened or becomes manipulative, for example. If you find yourself in a relationship where you can't talk about what's on your heart, you'll soon feel suffocated and trapped.

That doesn't mean that you can always talk about exactly how you feel. In therapy sessions I call this 'choosing your battles'. Not every battle is worth fighting. 'I have to learn to choose the right moment,' Wendy told me:

> I thought that when you were in a relationship, you could always talk about your feelings, immediately. But that's completely not the case! Sometimes I think he does or says something really stupid. And sometimes I bring it up later if it's really important, but sometimes I've just got to let go and forget about it. If necessary, I can always talk about it later, maybe even at a time where he can hear me better.

Choosing a good moment to talk about things is a very important relational skill. Once a client told about me about her fights with her boyfriend. She could rant at him terribly. He felt increasingly hurt and withdrew more and more, which, of course, just made her more angry. When I asked her about when these fights took place, she told me 'Yeah, it's really strange actually, but often just before dinner or going to sleep.' I looked at her. 'Hmm,' she mumbled, embarrassed, 'that actually sounds logical. Maybe we should eat or sleep first.' The number of fights between them began to lessen. Choose your fight and choose your moment.

'But how do I know if I'm in love with him "enough"?' Hannah looked at me desperately: 'I mean, I think he's fun and everything, and I know that he isn't perfect, but how do I know if what I feel for him is enough?' 'You have doubts?' I asked. 'Yes,' she sighed deeply. 'And what if you imagine your doubt as a monster. An orange one. Like a big fluffy, stuffed animal. Like in the book *Where the Wild Things Are.*[4] Can you do that?' 'Yeeees,' she said and hesitated for a bit, 'Yes I can.' 'How big is it?' 'Hey,' she said, relieved, 'actually not that big at all.'

'Okay, that's good,' I continued, 'and where is that orange monster? Between you and your boyfriend, or further away?' 'Between us' – furrowed brow: 'It's in the way. I can't see my boyfriend that well.' 'Exactly,' I observed, 'and where should it be? Where would be a better place for it to be? In a corner of the room, or on the balcony?' She began to laugh, relieved: 'On the balcony. That seems like a good place. It doesn't need to go away, I'm allowed to have doubts,' she continued, 'but not so many that it makes it difficult between us.'

Therefore it is very important in the first phase to give yourself time to learn, explore and discover by listening attentively to the other person. You're allowed to have doubts in this phase; it's even *healthy* to have them. Doubts help you to clarify what you want and don't want in a relationship, and help you keep a critical eye instead of being so blinded by infatuation that you dive right in. But we need to set limits to our doubts.

Hannah almost found herself in a panic because of her doubts. And through her panicked state her doubts grew even larger. In this way she learned that she was allowed to have doubts but that she could still continue in the relationship. This helped not only in discovering where she was in her relationship but in discovering who she was in a relationship.

PHASE 2: 'B' FOR 'BASIC COMMITMENT'

After some time spent examining the relationship and thinking it over, the moment of decision comes: 'Will I continue on in a relationship with this person or not?' Also in this phase you don't need to know or decide overnight whether or not you want to continue with this person. Time will tell. It's a decision that grows as you pray, think and talk about it.

The ethicist and theologian Stanley Hauerwas says 'You always marry the wrong person.'[5] You can't possibly make the same kind of informed choice as when you buy a washing machine or a car. You can carefully consider your options but a person is not a thing. A person is a complex and dynamic creation. You can't know now who someone will be in ten or twenty years but you can decide together that you will love each other again and again through those ten or twenty years, regardless of the circumstances.

In this sense, you'll also always marry the 'right one'. You will marry someone who is not perfect, and sooner or later you'll encounter those imperfections within your relationship. Our society always seems to be shouting 'Trade it in for something new!' when you don't like how things work out. Only sooner or later the 'new' also appears to have its own sort of brokenness. If you choose for someone, than that choice is for life.

There is freedom in marriage. Everyone who is happily married will tell you that he or she felt freer after making a decision. Of course it can sometimes be difficult to handle all of the practical responsibilities and rhythms within marriage, especially if you have children. But there is great freedom in the decision to choose another, and therefore choose to say 'no' to everyone else. It is a huge decision. 'A "yes" is often paired with many "nos"', my mentor told me when she heard that the man who is now my husband and I were in the decision-making phase of our relationship. You say 'yes' to one man, and with that you say 'no' to all your other 'options'.

'I'm stressing about a proposal,' I cried to my then boyfriend: 'I don't know if I would say "yes" if you proposed to me right now.' I was a heap of misery. My boyfriend laughed: 'I'm not planning that yet,' he said, 'and anyway you could just tell me: "I'm not ready yet"!' A client once said that she had said 'yes' to her boyfriend's proposal simply because she panicked in the moment. She kept wrestling with the ability to make her own choices within the relationship and because of this had a difficult time. Five years passed and she found herself in love with someone else. After a substantial relationship crisis, she decided to stay with her husband. They are still in therapy, but learning how to love each other in a new way. And he is helping her make her own choices.

Saying 'yes' from fear is far worse than saying 'no' because you don't yet know. Take enough time to talk about the important things. 'Do we want children? If so, when?' 'Do we agree about this?' 'How are we going to handle things financially, and what is our shared perspective about the future?' And the most important: 'How are we going to deal with challenges, if we're facing something and not on the same page?' Maybe this seems like a heavy topic of conversation for your courtship phase but these are the things that cause the greatest amount of conflict within marriages. It's sometimes difficult to be so serious, but very important.[6]

'I knew that she didn't want children,' Chris admitted, 'but we were 21 when we married, so I thought she'd change her mind in time. Now we're 36 and it appears that she still doesn't want children. And I don't want to wait any longer!' Their marriage was quickly falling apart. If they had seriously talked about this during their engagement, then it wouldn't be such a large problem now. Don't be naive about things but talk about them now so that you can make a good decision.

Incidentally, it's also tempting to live together in this phase. If you want to continue your relationship, if you're having a lot of fun, than why not live together? Research shows, however, that the chance of separation or divorce is significantly higher among those cohabitating.[7] This is called 'sliding versus deciding'. What usually happens when a really big decision isn't made to share their lives is that people regard themselves as free to back out when they don't 'feel it' any more. When they have grown into the habit of cohabitating, rather than when they have made a firm decision to marry, they have nothing to fall back on when things get rough; when they fall out of love. Without a clear moment of decision it is even more difficult to deal with challenges together. When the storms come to your relationship and you've never really said 'We're going to do this together, in good and in bad times', then the chance that one of you will walk away is greater.

Making a decision to be together is most apparent in a marriage proposal. Miriam said that when her boyfriend asked her to marry him, she didn't feel anything:

I thought: okay; now I'll feel these intense feelings of love that I thought I should feel by now. But no. Those feelings didn't really begin to happen until about three years after the wedding. I mean, I was always happy when we were together, you know, but not like I thought it would be. I didn't really have that 'wow' feeling. But now I have it more than ever. The moment of the proposal itself I was really overwhelmed. It was only a few days later that I began to feel really happy.

And men: never underestimate the value of a good proposal. It doesn't have to be huge or spectacular. 'I don't trust a man who makes a big deal of a marriage proposal,' says Julia Roberts in *Runaway Bride*: 'He seems as if he has something to hide.'[8] I don't believe that to be entirely true. Some men – or their potential wives – love big scenes and are especially extroverted. But a marriage proposal isn't about the show; it's about choosing that person. You're promising to care for the other person, even in the times when you don't even like him or her that much, even when they're sick or have a problem. You're undertaking an enormous responsibility, and this takes a great deal of love.

A good marriage proposal is clear and unambiguous, and therefore maybe also a bit overwhelming. If someone chooses you, then this is an enormous gift.

PHASE 3: 'C' FOR 'CHOICE'

After you've listened attentively and chosen to date someone exclusively, you're done with the work, right? Now you can plan the wedding. Sure, that can happen. But it is also a good idea to pause for a moment and see how you feel about your choice. Sometimes it's already very clear by the time you've chosen to date more seriously. But you're also not yet married; you can always change your mind. Jumping from a proposal into marriage can be too hasty and work against you. In addition, doubts can still return in all of the phases, and it's important to investigate if they're well founded or not.

'She had given earlier indications that she was never entirely sure,' Fred (32) admitted. 'But I didn't take them seriously. I wanted to get married so badly!' In retrospect, he realized he'd been moving too fast: 'I didn't want to know. If I'd only taken the time to listen to her.' His second-guessing girlfriend was actually searching for who she was. Two months before the wedding, she broke off the engagement. She told me:

> I was completely confused. In retrospect I see that I just wanted to *please* him, I wanted to keep him happy, and so I justified my feelings until one day, I couldn't deny them anymore. I realized that I'd stopped listening to myself. It was a big lesson to learn.

Three months after breaking off the engagement, they cautiously began to talk to each other. 'Eventually we learned what had gone wrong with us,' Fred told me. 'I turned out to be quite the dominant presence. Now I've learned to listen to her better, what she does and doesn't want. We now have new wedding plans but this time it is something that we're planning together!'

After the 'basic commitment' phase, they discovered that there was still more work to do. They decided to invest in the help of a counsellor. In the face of a delayed wedding, this might seem like a hard pill to swallow. However, the decision to get married is not about your image or glory but about the welfare of the other and taking good care of your relationship.

You may have to reconsider or change your original decision. Fred and his girlfriend got married after all, but you can also choose to break off the engagement completely. Sometimes in this phase you see things about the other person that you decide you really can't live with, and that he or she never intends to change. In the long term, it can be better for both you and the other person, saving you heartbreak or a failed marriage, if you leave while you can.

In the previous chapter I introduced the idea of an inverted funnel. If you use the funnel correctly with the narrow end pointing down, then the last phase before you make a final commitment is one in which you must continue to very carefully evaluate and critique the relationship. You can still walk away. Many people tell me 'I feel like such a loser in that I have two or three failed relationships/a broken engagement my name.' But better to have gone halfway towards marriage and turned around, than to have gone the whole way and made the wrong decision. Christian circles, especially, need to have more tolerance for broken relationships. Even marriage is not always fireproof. If something goes terribly wrong in a marriage, damaging one or both partners, then divorce can be a legitimate option.

Happily, however, for many couples the third phase is the calmest, in which you can simply enjoy each other and have fun with where you're at and where you're going. 'My engagement was probably the best time in our relationship,' mused Gertie, married three years. 'So calm and happy. I was finally past all of my doubts.'

As a man, when do you know the time is right to ask your girlfriend to marry you? My friend John talked about how he invited a good friend, also on his team, to discuss it with him. This friend had been married for years. He named five areas to think about when you're considering getting married:

- What is your heart telling you, including your emotions?
- What about your mind?
- What does God say?
- What about the people around you?
- How do your experiences with this person speak into this decision?

The first two questions relate to yourself. What do *you* want? Are your heart and mind in agreement or aren't they? Your mind might be saying 'Yes, but . . .', while your emotions say 'Go for it!' Or you may have some feelings of anxiety but these then become less important if, in your heart of hearts, you feel sure you want to marry this person and you have carefully thought everything through and believe it is the right decision.

You also need to involve God and your friends in your decision. How can you involve God in your choice? It will be essential for Christians to take every aspect of the relationship to God in careful prayer, seeking his wisdom and guidance. This may well partly come through God's using the other people in your life to shine a light on your planned commitment.

Your friends have watched your relationship for a while now and can probably tell you whether or not they like the two of you together. If he or she doesn't click with all or most of your friends, this is most likely a bad sign. If they're not encouraging you in your relationship, there's probably a good reason. They aren't there to hurt you but to think through the relationship with you. If your friends and family are encouraging you to go for it, you should also take this seriously. If they're cheering you on, then you're probably making a good decision.

PHASE 4: 'D' FOR 'DECISION'

Finally, it is good to think over what your experiences together have been. You've been together for some time, and if it's been a good relationship, then you've seen each other in all sorts of circumstances: at a party but also the morning after; in stylish clothes and old ones; under stress and in total relaxation. You don't need to know every detail of someone's life up until the point you met to know who someone is. But you do learn a lot by simply being together. What do your experiences tell you?

How someone reacts to stress, for example, is very informative. People often say that you need to do chores around the house and go camping together before you make the decision to marry. It's important to know if someone 'flips out' or shuts down under pressure. And then there's the question of how you handle it together. Can you solve it together or not?

If you still have doubts, the following exercise from the Benedictine Christian spiritual tradition may help. Make a decision and live for three days with that decision. So say you decide to marry the person you're dating. Don't say anything yet to him or her, but imagine that this is a reality for a full three days. How does it feel? Are you relieved, happy even? Or is something nagging you? If so, what could it be? Take your thoughts and feelings seriously and bring them before God. Then take the next three days to imagine the alternative. How are things different?

Recently I heard a beautiful story about a woman who prayed that God would give her an image of her future partner. She received a vision where she saw a stone. Two years later she was seriously dating a man with whom she found herself falling more deeply in love. But she still had doubts. One day they were talking about future plans, and just then he took out a stone and held it out to her. 'Maybe this is strange, but I've saved this for two years. I found it on the beach and somehow thought, "Maybe this has something to do with my future wife." But I have no idea what.' She burst into tears and told him the story about her vision of the stone.

Most couples don't need such a dramatic story to confirm their love for the other. It can certainly happen but it's not necessary. Ultimately your decision to marry is above all *your own decision*, and therefore also your own responsibility. In the times when the marriage becomes difficult, it's that moment of decision to which you return.

SEX AND BOUNDARIES

By this point in your relationship together you may have to reconsider your physical boundaries. What are good boundaries in engagement? Where the boundaries lie is a very personal question, something to be decided between the two of you. The most important issue is that you stay in continual conversation with each other, whatever your choices are, and that you're careful to stay on the same page.

The topic should always be available for discussion. If all is well in your relationship, physical intimacy grows along with your relationship. As long as you're able to grow emotionally, socially and spiritually towards each other in a balanced way, then you can also allow the physical intimacy to grow.

Sexually speaking, you need to talk more than you practise. Talking things over with someone already requires a certain level of intimacy. Why wouldn't you ever talk with a one-night stand about sex? It would seem inappropriate, maybe even awkward. But you need to be able to talk about sex with the person with whom you've agreed to share your life. While you're engaged, the more you know about where the other person's limits are, and what they want and don't want, the easier it will be to talk openly about sex and boundaries once you're married. This needs to be an ongoing conversation in every relationship.

If you find yourself stumbling around in this area of sexual boundaries, talk with your team about it – or ask someone on your team to be your accountability partner, someone who can help keep you responsible. Even if waiting to have sex until marriage is something that's really important to you, it can sometimes be difficult to stick to your boundaries. Knowing that you're accountable to someone helps you to be more intentional with your partner and respecting of your agreed boundaries.

If you're still looking for clear rules, such as 'Keep your panties on', be assured that rules alone aren't enough to protect you from going too far. You need to use your head, especially when things heat up. Not drinking alcohol might be a big help! Another helpful tool is the chapter on sexual boundaries in the book *Boundaries in Dating* by Henry Cloud and John Townsend.[9] The best foundation is still this: talk about everything! If something is too embarrassing to say out loud, then why would you dare to do it?

LAST BUT NOT LEAST

I once heard a friend say: 'Planning your wedding is the first big project that you work on together.' Planning a wedding together can also be an incredibly tough job. Some couples agree on every decision from the beginning but more often a lot of give and take is needed. If you find yourself in the latter category, cheer up: it's good practice. You'll also need to make decisions together later in marriage, maybe in the raising of your children, for example. The earlier you can practise this, the better.

The engagement period can be exactly when you can get taken over by all the practical things and forget to keep talking about where the two of you are relationally. Or you might find you're avoiding some more challenging topics of conversation because you're busy. At this stage it's extremely important to keep the essence of marriage in mind: it's the bringing together of two lives rather than just planning a really good party.

If you've decided to get married, a marriage preparation course can be useful. Many people who've done this sort of course have been positive about their experiences. Every now and then a couple discover that there are fundamental differences between them that can't be solved, and the engagement is broken off; but better a broken engagement than a broken marriage – it's never easy but is survivable.

I was recently at a wedding where the words 'difficult', 'trouble' and 'do your best' were used quite frequently during the ceremony. However, marriage is neither more difficult nor less work than being single. Above all, marriage is simply another phase of life – not necessarily better or worse, but if it's as it's intended, usually more fun than being alone.

A sign of a good relationship is that your connection with God, yourself and the people around you is growing, not shrinking. In this third phase, when the storm of doubts and questions has calmed and the dust settled, you begin to see that a healthy relationship is a very good thing. You see that it's more fun and meaningful to eat with someone, to wake up next to someone, to go on vacation with someone. And you find yourself saying 'Life with you is even better.'

QUESTIONS FOR FURTHER REFLECTION

- When do you decide to date exclusively?
- Are you able to be an attentive listener in your relationship? Can your intended partner listen attentively to you?
- When do you decide to make plans to marry and how do you decide on timing?
- What are your sexual boundaries during both your dating and engagement periods?

ASSIGNMENTS

- Take the time in each phase of exclusive dating (according to the ABC phases of: *a*ttentive listening; *b*asis (the foundation of your relationship); *c*hoice (will you stay by your decision to be together?).
- Discuss with your team: Is this person a good fit? Why or why not?
- Talk about the important things with each other – children, finances and so on – at the right time.
- If you have plans to marry, take a Marriage Preparation Course and read *Rules of Engagement* by Katharine and Richard Hill.[10]

Appendix
Date evaluation sheet

If you've been on a date, it can really help to process the date using a form like the one in Table 2, which you can copy into a notepad. It can also be useful for your team members, so that they're familiar with which kinds of questions they can ask you if you've been on a date.

If you don't have an answer to a question, ask yourself why not. Have you simply not got to that point in the relationship (and that can be because you've only known each other a short time)? Or is there another reason?

Table 2 Date evaluation sheet

	Pros	*Cons*
General information about the date (time, location, activity, etc.)		
How I relate to this person		
About the other person (character qualities, values, boundaries, etc.)		

Notes

1 CONNECTING TO GOD

1 For resources, see <www.hudmcwilliams.com>.

2 Lori Gottlieb, *Mr Good Enough: The Case for Choosing a Real Man over Holding Out for Mr Perfect* (London: Collins, 2010), p. 7.

3 *Jerry Maguire* (TriStar Pictures, 1996).

4 Plato, *The Symposium*, trans. C. Gill (London: Penguin, 1999), pp. 22ff.

5 Joshua Harris, *I Kissed Dating Goodbye* (Sisters, OR: Multnomah, 1997), p. 18.

6 *Visie*, magazine of the Evangelische Omroep – <www.eo.nl/magazines/visie/artikel-detail/ik-ben-vrijgezel-prima-toch>.

7 Mark Regnerus, *Premarital Sex in America: How Young Americans Meet, Mate, and Think about Marrying* (Oxford; New York: Oxford University Press, 2011), p. 139.

8 This research can be found at <www.singlechristians.co.uk>.

9 Timothy Keller with Kathy Keller, *The Meaning of Marriage: Facing the Complexities of Commitment with the Wisdom of God* (New York: Dutton, 2011), pp. 40–1.

10 You can find the Christian Connection research on the website of Engage – <www.engage-mcmp.org.uk>.

2 CONNECTING TO YOURSELF

1 This is the short version of what Sue Johnson in her excellent book *Hold Me Tight* calls 'the dance', when she speaks about the interaction patterns between couples – Sue Johnson, *Hold Me Tight: Your Guide to the Most Successful Approach to Building Loving Relationships* (London: Piatkus, 2011).

2 Meg Jay, *The Defining Decade: Why Your Twenties Matter and How to Make the Most of Them Now* (New York: Twelve, 2012).

3 Henry Cloud, *How to Get a Date Worth Keeping: Be Dating in Six Months or Your Money Back* (Grand Rapids, MI: Zondervan, 2005), p. 42. I strongly recommend that you read this for more information and advice on how practically to achieve the goal of the assignment.

4 Henry Cloud and John Townsend, *Safe People: How to Find Relationships that Are Good for You and Avoid Those that Aren't* (Grand Rapids, MI: Zondervan, 1995).

5 HopefulGirl, *Would Like to Meet: The Real-Life Diary of a 30-Something Christian Woman Looking for Love* (Abingdon: Bible Reading Fellowship, 2013). This quote can also be found in one of her blogs at Christian Connection – <http://blog.christianconnection.com/shopping-for-love-dont-go-home-empty-handed>.

6 Lori Gottlieb, *Mr Good Enough: The Case for Choosing a Real Man over Holding Out for Mr Perfect* (London: Collins, 2010), ch. 2.

7 The website of Christian Vision for Men has a section called Porn Free, but the resources are relevant for women too – <www.cvm.org.uk/porn-free>.

8 Jay, *Defining Decade*, p. xxvi.

9 Jay, *Defining Decade*, p. 71.

3 CONNECTING TO A COMMUNITY

1 Henry Cloud, *How to Get a Date Worth Keeping: Be Dating in Six Months or Your Money Back* (Grand Rapids, MI: Zondervan, 2005), pp. 82ff.

2 More information on this research can be found at <https://archive.
   org/details/PsychogenicD>.

3 From the DVD *Extreme Dating Makeover* by Henry Cloud, available
   at the Cloud/Townsend webshop – <https://store.cloudtownsend.
   com>.

4 Cloud, *How to Get a Date Worth Keeping*; quote is title of ch. 16,
   pp. 106–8.

5 As described in Helen E. Fisher et al., 'Reward, Addiction, and
   Emotion Regulation Systems Associated With Rejection in Love',
   Journal of Neurophysiology 104:1, 2010, pp. 51– 60. Also very interesting is Helen Fisher's 2008 TED Talk video, 'The Brain in Love' –
   <www.youtube.com/watch?v=OYfoGTIG7pY>.

6 Cloud, *How to Get a Date Worth Keeping*, p. 89.

7 *Vanilla Sky* (Paramount Pictures, 2001).

8 Timothy Keller with Kathy Keller, *The Meaning of Marriage: Facing
   the Complexities of Commitment with the Wisdom of God* (New York:
   Dutton, 2011), pp. 219–36.

9 Keller, *Meaning of Marriage*, p. 302.

10 The film *Arranged* (Cicala Filmworks, 2007) is about modern match-
   making among devout Jewish couples in New York.

11 In the UK, the Engage Network is supporting just this, to help
   churches empower people more when it comes to singleness, dating
   and relationships. And they're doing a fabulous job – <www.engage-
   mcmp.org.uk>.

4 CONNECTING TO THE OTHER PERSON

1 This is a fairly simplified summary of the Big Five theory of personality – the theory that made most sense to me out of all of the
   theoretical views I read during my studies of psychology. One of
   the basic works on personality development is Jess Feist and Gregory
   J. Feist, *Theories of Personality* (Boston, MA: McGraw-Hill, 1998).

2 I'd always advise Myra and friends to read Lori Gottlieb, *Mr Good Enough: The Case for Choosing a Real Man over Holding Out for Mr Perfect* (London: Collins, 2010).

3 See <http://en.wikipedia.org/wiki/Aish_HaTorah>. The rabbi and his wife, Sue, have even written a book about it and patented the method: Yaacov Deyo and Sue Deyo, *Speed Dating: The Smarter, Faster Way to Lasting Love* (New York: HarperCollins, 2002).

4 Barry Schwartz, *The Paradox of Choice: Why More Is Less* (New York: Ecco, 2003). You can also watch his fascinating 2005 TED Talk at TED global – <www.ted.com/talks/barry_schwartz_on_the_paradox_of_choice>.

5 Henry Cloud, *How to Get a Date Worth Keeping: Be Dating in Six Months or Your Money Back* (Grand Rapids, MI: Zondervan, 2005); quote is title of ch. 16, pp. 106–8.

6 Ellen Fein and Sherrie Schneider, *The Rules: Time-tested Secrets for Capturing the Heart of Mr. Right* (New York: Warner Books, 1995).

5 FINDING YOUR MATCH: NOW WHAT?

1 Timothy Keller with Kathy Keller, *The Meaning of Marriage: Facing the Complexities of Commitment with the Wisdom of God* (New York: Dutton, 2011), p. 216.

2 Keller, *Meaning of Marriage*, p. 213.

3 In the DVD series The Marriage Preparation Course, accompanying Nicky Lee and Sila Lee, *The Marriage Book* (London: Alpha International, 2000).

4 Maurice Sendak, *Where the Wild Things Are* (New York: Harper & Row, 1963).

5 Stanley Hauerwas, ed. John Berkman and Michael Cartwright, *The Hauerwas Reader* (Durham, NC: Duke University Press, 2001), p. 524. Also in Stanley Hauerwas, *A Community of Character: Toward*

a Constructive Christian Social Ethic (Notre Dame, IN: University of Notre Dame Press, 1981).

6 A book that can help you prepare is Gary Chapman, *Things I Wished I'd Known before We Got Married* (Chicago, IL: Northfield Publishing, 2010).

7 Scott M. Stanley, Galena Kline Rhoades and Howard J. Markman call it the issue of 'sliding versus deciding' in their article 'Sliding versus Deciding: Inertia and the Premarital Cohabitation Effect' (*Family Relations* 55:4, 2006, pp. 499–509). You can read more about sliding or deciding in Meg Jay, *The Defining Decade: Why Your Twenties Matter and How to Make the Most of Them Now* (New York: Twelve, 2012) and in Harry Benson's research in the UK, which can be found on the Marriage Foundation website – <www.marriagefoundation.org.uk/ research>.

8 *Runaway Bride* (Paramount Pictures, 1999).

9 Henry Cloud and John Townsend, *Boundaries in Dating: How Healthy Choices Grow Healthy Relationships* (Grand Rapids, MI: Zondervan, 2000).

10 Katharine Hill and Richard Hill, *Rules of Engagement: How to Plan a Successful Wedding. How to Build a Marriage that Lasts*, 2nd edn (Oxford: Lion Hudson, 2009).

Further reading

BOOKS

Abbema, Aukelien van, *Single in de Kerk: De Mythes en de Mogelijkheden* (Amsterdam: Ark Media, 2012).

Chediak, Alex (ed.), *5 Paths to the Love of Your Life: Defining your Dating Style* (Colorado Springs, CO: TH1NK Books, 2005).

Cloud, Henry, *How to Get a Date Worth Keeping: Be Dating in Six Months or Your Money Back* (Grand Rapids, MI: Zondervan, 2005).

Cloud, Henry and Townsend, John, *Boundaries in Dating: How Healthy Choices Grow Healthy Relationships* (Grand Rapids, MI: Zondervan, 2000).

Cloud, Henry and Townsend, John, *Safe People: How to Find Relationships that Are Good for You and Avoid Those that Aren't* (Grand Rapids, MI: Zondervan, 1995).

Fein, Ellen and Schneider, Sherrie, *The Rules: Time-tested Secrets for Capturing the Heart of Mr. Right* (New York: Warner Books, 1995).

Gottlieb, Lori, *Mr Good Enough: The Case for Choosing a Real Man over Holding Out for Mr Perfect* (London: Collins, 2010).

Gray, John, *Mars and Venus on a Date: A Guide for Navigating the 5 Stages of Dating to Create a Loving and Lasting Relationship* (New York: Harper-Perennial, 1999).

Hall, Paula, *Confronting Porn* (Durham: Naked Truth Resources, 2016).

Harris, Joshua, *I Kissed Dating Goodbye* (Sisters, OR: Multnomah, 1997).

Hauerwas, Stanley, *A Community of Character: Toward a Constructive Christian Social Ethic* (Notre Dame, IN: University of Notre Dame Press, 1981).

HopefulGirl, *Would Like to Meet: The Real-Life Diary of a 30-Something Christian Woman Looking for Love* (Abingdon: Bible Reading Fellowship, 2013).

Jay, Meg, *The Defining Decade: Why Your Twenties Matter and How to Make the Most of Them Now* (New York: Twelve, 2012).

Johnson, Sue, *Hold Me Tight: Your Guide to the Most Successful Approach to Building Loving Relationships* (London: Piatkus, 2011).

Keller, Timothy with Keller, Kathy, *The Meaning of Marriage: Facing the Complexities of Commitment with the Wisdom of God* (New York: Dutton, 2011).

Klinenberg, Eric, *Going Solo: The Extraordinary Rise and Surprising Appeal of Living Alone* (New York: Penguin, 2012).

Lee, Nicky and Lee, Sila, *The Marriage Book* (London: Alpha International, 2000).

Nijs, Piet, *Gesluierde Eros: Seksuele Verveling en Erotische Burn-out* (Mechelen: Kluwer, 2004).

WEBSITES

There are many great resources on dating on the website of Henry Cloud and John Townsend – <www.cloudtownsend.com>.

Dating advice blogs of E-harmony or Christian Connection are often helpful on the more practical issues – <www.eharmony.com/blog>; <www.christianconnection.com>.

Informative and very funny short clips on dating and relationships by Joy Eggerichs can be found on – <www.loveandrespectnow.com>.

On the website of the Christian Associates psychologist Hud McWilliams there is a very insightful lecture on dating and relationship formation ('Finding True Love and Making it Last') – <www.hudmcwilliams. com/video>.

For marriage preparation material from Prepare/Enrich go to – <www.prepare-enrich.com>.

I love the Marriage Preparation Course as developed by Nicky and Sila Lee of Alpha International's Relationship Central – <www.relationshipcentral.org>. That's where my inspiration for developing a dating course first came from.

For a Christian charity based in the UK that 'opens eyes and frees lives' from the damaging impact of pornography, go to – <http://thenakedtruthproject.com>. For a US charity that is tackling the issue of pornography, go to – <http://fightthenewdrug.org>.

Leabharlanna Poibli Chathair Bhaile Átha Cliath
Dublin City Public Libraries